Using (Other) People's (Money)

How to invest in property

Third Edition

— VICKI WUSCHE —

Using Other People's Money How to invest in property

Third Edition

—— Vicki Wusche ——

Using Other People's Money: How to invest in property
© Vicki Wusche 2014
ISBN 978-1-909116-36-8
First published in 2010 by Vizzi Publishing
Second edition published in 2012 by SRA Books
This third edition published in 2014 by SRA Books

Printed in the UK by TJ International, Padstow

Vicki Wusche
The Shed
St Peters Road
Uxbridge, UB8 3SB

Vicki@Wusche-Associates.co.uk
Skype: Vicki.Wusche
www.TheSourcersApprentice.com

Liability disclaimer

The information contained in this book has been gathered and collated from the experiences of the author. Every effort has been made to make sure the details are accurate. However, they are experiences and by that nature, and the fact that they have been gathered into a book, means that they will be in the past as you read this.

It is vital that you take this information and check its relevancy to your personal situation and to the market place right now. We have been through six of the most unprecedented years in the economy, all rulebooks have been torn up and no one knows what the future holds. It is the lessons of the present that carry us forward.

Please take this information, learn from the mistakes, benefit from the successes and, above all, carve your own future in the shape you desire. Deals are easy to find but hard to buy without finance; identify your personal sources of finance and build a cashflow portfolio now.

Contents

Foreword

You have to take your hat off to Vicki Wusche. She didn't enter the property world at the top floor, but at ground level. As a single mum, with two daughters, living on benefits in social housing.

It's fair to say, then, that her CV is a little different from that of most other people listed among the *The Telegraph* Top 25 Property Movers and Shakers.

That said, what has got her to where she is today, is the degree of seriousness with which she takes the whole business of property investment. When you start with not a lot, an investment can't just be a random punt in the dark, it has to be a carefully thought out and targeted decision.

It's a mark of the care she takes, that rather than just reprinting the last version of this book, she has rewritten the text, in the light of the recent, turbulent conditions in the housing market.

Having read what she has to say, you don't, of course, have to plunge straight in after the Property Mermaid and start accumulating properties. But you should, at least, have acquired the confidence to put a toe into the water.

Christopher Middleton
Freelance Writer
The Telegraph Property Section

About Vicki Wusche and this third revised edition

Property investment is a serious business that requires the investor to maintain focus on their specific reason for investing while being constantly aware of the changing economic climate around them. This third edition of *Using Other People's Money: How to invest in property* has been radically rewritten, completely rejecting some of the previous strategies in light of the current economic climate. There are six brand new chapters and a further nine that have been completely rewritten.

Vicki Wusche, The Property Mermaid

Any business environment, if providing opportunities, will by nature be dynamic. When I wrote the first edition of this book in 2010, the previous two years had been chaotic. We had just experienced unprecedented changes in lender and bank confidence, the economy and the housing market. Everything that existing investors knew was thrown into the air. Many investors spent time and money 'trying' to find 'new' ways of investing. In fact, they were just avoiding the reality of the situation. Banks no longer wanted to lend 100% of the loan amount. We had to find a new way of doing business. The first edition reviewed those strategies through my experience and those of colleagues, in an effort to make sense of that new world and all the ideas being developed. The second edition added another 18 months' experience into the mix. Between 2010 and 2012 I continued to buy investment properties for myself and clients. I worked with other mentoring clients (some new to property and others very experienced) to look at how we could easily make more money from property – this, in turn, prompted my second book, *Make More Money from Property: From investor thinking to a business mindset*.

Now pundits are speculating that the market will rise. I believe it will dramatically change and that those changes will not be easy to predict. Borrowing money remains a challenge, especially with the introduction of the Mortgage Market Review in the residential lending arena.

And while confidence in the general population is bolstered by government incentives and media speculation – the economics of supply and demand lead me to worry about the depth and strength of any real recovery, when the majority of the population have not seen a real increase in salary or disposable income. Just how can property prices increase and remain affordable?

Why am I rewriting this book? Because this book has been incredibly popular over the last four years and received great reviews stating that it is a valuable resource. There has been so much change that rather than just reprint a book that was two years old, I decided to rewrite it. There is still such a huge demand from investors, new and experienced, to understand what is working well and what is not. And so there should be. Because without continual professional and business development, our portfolios would stop providing us with the financial freedom that we desire!

In recent months I have been giving talks on 'The Business of Investing' (in fact I am in the process of writing my fourth book under that title). If we are genuinely seeing the start of long term sustainable economic recovery and an increase in property prices then new strategies need to be considered (not necessarily brand new ideas, just some of those out of favour for the last 4–6 years).

What I have personally witnessed is a lot of people rushing to jump on the property bandwagon without clearly understanding all of the implications, consequences and risks.

My aim with this new edition of *Using Other People's Money: How to invest in property* is to clearly layout the financial implications and the lifestyle consequences of each strategy in order that you can make the best possible and financially strategic decisions. Remember whatever else happens we still have an election on the near horizon and with that all the politicking and media manipulation the parties can muster. Who can you trust? What information is fact and what is just hype?

Let me begin by explaining how I started my journey into property investment, so you can see that everything in this book is possible. The difference between the three editions is that I have even more experience to share.

In the following chapters I will explain how to choose the best strategy for you and your family, the tools and strategies you need to be successful and why identifying your own sources of personal finance is crucial to building a cashflowing portfolio.

First, to introduce myself

I invest for a lifestyle

I have come to be known as 'The Property Mermaid'. This is because my desire to scuba dive all the warm waters of the world has always been a key goal and driving force in my life – even before property. Now The Property Mermaid has become a metaphor for my life, my vision and my goals. To me The Property Mermaid is the image of a lifestyle that enables me to combine an income-generating business with quality time with my family and friends. It is an image of happiness, joy and freedom; a reminder.

Your metaphor (key words, or images) might include other sports, music or art. Whether you are The Golfing Hippy, The Time Wizard, The Polar Explorer or The Gentle Dog Walker, it is crucial to understand what life and lifestyle you want. Even celebrities have these 'fame name' monikers (The Naked Chef, Super Nanny), these brand names are actually just words that help you easily remember their purpose, values, passion or business. What would yours be? (And you can have different ones at different times of your life.)

It is not enough to just want to make more money – for what purpose? If you don't know what you want to do with your money then £10 extra is money; £1,000 is more money but it might not be enough ... because you are not clear why you want the money.

Once I understood why I wanted more money I had a reason to learn how the money system worked. This enabled me to learn even more including the concept of leverage, and the advantage of leveraging other people's money. That was when I was able to create a business and lifestyle that let me indulge both passions – business and property investment as well as scuba diving and henceforth live the life of The Property Mermaid.

Property investment can enable you to live the life of your dreams. This book can open the door to financial freedom, through a property portfolio you never thought of. Our biggest challenge is to overcome years of conditioning by our parents and school that encourages us to get a job, buy a house and live happily ever after. Yes, I want that too, but the difference is that I have recognised that I need to invest my money and make it work alongside me to achieve that dream. Not hope that a government pension will keep me warm in my old age!

Since the publication of the first edition, I have started a number of associated property ventures, including a training brand called TheSourcersApprentice.com which offers training materials for investors – new and experienced.

ThePropertySourcers.com offers a hands-free cashflowing portfolio service to bespoke clients.

As I started to write the first edition, I realised that my core principle and driving force is to share knowledge. I guess I will always be a teacher at heart. Therefore, the training business, this book, my second book *Make More Money from Property: From investor thinking to a business mindset*, webinars, strategy sessions, online courses and other training materials are enabling me to share my experience with other property investors, new and experienced, by combining my teaching skills with business acumen. Understanding property as a business is vital to your success.

The Property Sourcers evolved into my primary focus over the last two years. I have been focused on working with cash-rich investors to increase the return on their investments by buying and controlling property. I share my expertise and knowledge to enable them to create financial freedom by leveraging the financial resources that they did not necessarily appreciate they had. I now have a business team that work with me and, of course, business systems that enable us to buy and convert at least two properties per month for clients. In 2014 and beyond I aim to increase this capacity through my work with excellent mentees that will progress to become new business partners. More about them later.

My first brush with property came when I was 25 and worked for a mortgage broker. I had always looked at property, noticed it and wondered about it. I loved the job – the organising and the numbers, the talking to people, and helping them to achieve their dreams of owning their own home.

Property kept tapping me on the shoulder and finally I started to listen. In 2001, my sister and I decided to invest in property. This was an important decision, made more challenging because of the journey I had already travelled. To summarise and for completeness, there had been a marriage, two beautiful daughters, isolation, bullying, my ex-husband's bankruptcy, the forced sale of our home just before it could be repossessed (while I was eight months' pregnant with one of my daughters) and then finally a divorce.

As a single mum with two children under three years living on benefits in social housing, I started university and a happier, more empowered life.

It took three years to agree on a property investment strategy with my sister. I just knew property was a good idea, but I didn't have any property experience or training. My sister and I were lucky. We met a man who turned out to be honourable and very good at his job. We started investing with a pooled pot of money. There have been so many people that I have met over the last six years that have fallen into a financial disaster because they trusted the wrong person and invested in the wrong (foreign and UK) property scheme. We were very lucky!

We later remortgaged and bought more property. It could have so easily been different. I had no experience and no training – no clue in fact, just a feeling. So the journey started and the London portfolio was developed.

Yes, I fell off the wagon. Yes, I had a studio flat in Estonia. Then luck intervened again. In 2007, I studied some of the most powerful and mind-expanding courses possible. Since 1993, I had been a university lecturer, completed my first degree and had studied a Master's degree, but I had never heard stuff like this. I learnt that I could control my own mind and my own destiny just by the choices I made and the things I focused on – it was mind blowing!

The icing on the cake was to finally understand the power of money, investing and leverage. Up to now, I had already been doing all of the above, but more by luck rather than design. Now I consciously understood the strategies and techniques and over the next four years the result of all this mind enabling learning was to create a new cashflowing property portfolio, financial freedom, two new property businesses, three Amazon bestselling books and finally in 2013 to be recognised as one of the UK's top 25 most influential people in property according to *The Telegraph*.[1]

Now the hard-core property bit

In 2008, as I finally left the world of personal development, after months of training I started to see things differently. One of the crucial lessons I have learned over the last six years is that it is vital you know what you want to learn from a training session. Understand the outcomes – are they what you want? If the answer is yes, do the people delivering the course have the current real-world experience you need?

When did they last buy a property and what strategy did they use? Finally, how much does the course cost and is it value for money? With so many companies out there, you do not have to pay the £10,000s I paid! I didn't know that when I started. So I ended up attending a three-day free course at which I increased my credit card limits as part of a class exercise and miraculously found myself with the available credit to buy the next course they were selling for £20,000.

I have met so many people who have spent thousands of pounds and yet still have not invested in property or sold a deal. They are still attending courses – actually they are afraid. I have felt like that and I am sure you have too – it's natural.

Why are they afraid? I believe it is either because they are not learning the relevant strategies to help them start, or they do not have the 'right mindset' (dreadful phrase, I know). By this, I mean that they have not aligned their goals and their values in a way that will enable them to take dramatic and unstoppable action – leading to financial freedom. I will spend a whole chapter helping you to prepare for property success.

After my first three days of training, I went out and put everything I knew and understood into practice. By the time we started our next training course some three months later, we were just about to complete on our first property. The 'house from hell'. That's unfair, the house is lovely. However, the seller was mad, the no money down deal was a nightmare, the market volatile, Mortgage Express was just about to close down and rates were rising – a really scary time to start a new career.

---

1   http://www.telegraph.co.uk/property/propertymarket/10352943/Property-power-list-2013-25-movers-and-shakers.html?frame=2691414

It got worse.

From August to November 2008, I didn't manage to buy anything else. House purchases fell through because sellers pulled out, surveyors down valued, there were structural faults, poor relationships with the estate agents or I was gazumped by other investors. I lost confidence. I was networking, but I had no real property friends, mentors or support.

I was out of the training loop. I wasn't earning money. I thought I was a professional investor – I had done the training – why wasn't I getting the properties? I even had the 'right mindset'!

What changed?

I made the decision in December 2008 that I was either going to get successful at this or go back to work, and I didn't want to do that – I had a lifestyle mapped out, holidays to take. If I failed, I would make myself get a job at a supermarket stacking shelves – that certainly became a great deterrent.

In January 2009, Bob, my life and business partner, and I worked with a coach to help repair my confidence. I came to understand that I was 'trying' to do too many things. Alongside investing in property, I had joined a multi-level marketing (MLM) business. My attention was divided.

From January 2009 onwards, I listened to my coach and I focused on what I wanted to achieve, on what I was doing and on what I was learning. Everything was about property and within four weeks I had stopped the other distracting activities and I had another two deals on the table.

I continued to buy, on average, two properties a month for the whole of 2009. By the end of 2009, I had a sourcing business doing, effectively, more of the same – buying cashflowing properties for myself and now for fee-paying clients.

Then, in January 2010, I lost focus by writing the first edition of this book! The book became a massive task – not the writing so much as the processes of editing and publishing the book – something I knew nothing about. In 2010 I only bought six properties!

The following chapters will cover everything that I have discovered through practice between 2009 and 2014. They are the techniques needed to buy property in the current economic climate and the 'looming boom'!

So why write a book?

Over the last five years I have personally spoken at a number of property events and courses. In January 2010 alone, I spoke to over 600 people at various events. In 2012 I was invited to give two key note talks at The Great British Business Show. During 2013–14 I travelled the country sharing my story and understanding of property.

The most common question I am still asked is: 'I don't have any money, how can I invest in property?' The answer is, of course, to use other people's money – and that's why I decided to write this book, to share with as many people as possible the knowledge of how to invest in property. This third edition of the book, like the first two editions, will help you to recognise how important it is to know how you are going to fund your property investments and to develop those crucial strategies. Where this edition adds massive value is by helping you to recognise the relationship between strategy, outcome and your personal life and lifestyle goal.

What are the crucial finance strategies?

In the 'good old days' all an investor had to do was find a property and use Mortgage Express to give them a same-day remortgage. They then withdrew all the equity on day one, leaving none of their own cash in the deal. It was that simple to buy a property and literally use none of your own money.

I now believe that led to a lot of bad investment decisions, a lot of laziness. Investors bought 'off-plan' flats that were overvalued by developers and surveyors alike. They over leveraged the properties – taking out high mortgages which left them vulnerable and, for some, over exposed as the prices inevitably started to crumble. Worse, in many cases they didn't even consider how the mortgages would be paid. Yes, by the rent of course, but what about the business basics of supply and demand?

Soon overpriced, over-mortgaged properties in large city-centre blocks were coming up for tenancy renewals and it became a tenant's market place. The result? A dramatic fall in the value of these rents, combined with increasing mortgage rates – a recipe for bankruptcy and months of sheer financial hell.

At one point an investor friend was paying £6,000 in mortgage costs out of his own pocket! Now that is not sustainable investing by anybody's measure.

Sadly, a lot of investors still pursue strategies where their aim is to leave no money in a deal – in effect to be 100% mortgaged. This level of gearing is dangerous in my opinion. We need healthy portfolios with equity in the deal to cover the impact of further house price falls and the inevitable increase in interest rates. Your focus needs to be on cashflow not on the size of your portfolio. This risk analysis may be hard for some to accept with all the media and Office of National Statistics (ONS) reporting a property boom[2], but we have been here before. Be careful!

Leaving none of your own money in a deal might sound appealing as you can buy lots of properties, but you will have lots of debt to service too. Why not have fewer properties with a lot of cashflow that covers the cost of borrowing with plenty to spare? Why not work out how much you need in cashflow and buy that many houses?

It is more difficult to buy investment properties now. Why is this, if the deals are still relatively easy to find? Principally, because the lenders have realised that they were lending money on property without proper safeguards in place. If the property value fell or the investors could not repay the debt, then there was no cushion to enable the lender to recoup the debt.

Some people say that if the deal is good, then the money will come. I believe that the money comes from the sources you have identified and the strategies you have developed.

This third edition goes one step further in helping you to make money from your property knowledge. It will show you some of the key business principles I have applied over the last two years to grow my business and income even further.

So who is this book for?

Well, *you*. Whether you are new to property investing and not sure how to start when you don't have a bottomless pot of cash to deposit in property, or whether you are an investor experienced in the old ways of working, and maybe even have a highly leveraged portfolio, I believe this book will be useful. New or experienced, I know you will find a gem in this book, a new way of investing or a better understanding of a strategy where you had not

---

2   http://www.bbc.co.uk/news/business-27484221

previously seen the benefit. Below are just a handful of the hundreds of comments I received about the first two editions.

'I saw Vicki talk last night at a property networking event, bought her book and woke up early today to read it. I was so excited – I have properties already, but the money from banks has run out. So I have been struggling with how to get back into the property market with absolutely no money. People I talk to don't believe it can be done, but Vicki is a very ethical person and she knows her stuff. If you have been using the old "I don't have enough money to get into property" excuse, then you now have nowhere to hide as Vicki explains how *everyone* can get into property. One of the best property books I have read!'

Fiona H

'I've just finished your "manual" on how to raise money. Have put it straight to work and raised £50k from a neighbour who recently sold an inherited house. It also gave me the idea/confidence to ask the divorced owner of a property I am currently buying what he intends on doing with the money! (He had already bought another property.) He came to the conclusion that it would be better to invest his £100k with me. You are right when you say it is a huge responsibility. Thanks for being there.'

Francis D

'I must say your books have been an eye opener and full of nuggets of wisdom on how to create wealth from property through leveraging to become financially free now and for the future. There's so much in the pages of both books its frankly mind-blowing and I can't thank you enough for the advice given. If you don't mind we may want to engage your services as a coach for the business as without doubt you are one of the most knowledgeable persons in the property business and your portfolio building format seems the most sensible and least complicated.'

Frederick A

'A lot of the things you said in your book struck a chord and have set me thinking in ways I'd not previously considered. In fact the last couple of days I've thought of little else, especially your point about asking myself why I'm doing this and what it is I actually want. In the past I've definitely been guilty of being too vague with my goals, and I'm finding that (even after this short a time, three days) drilling down into the detail of what it is I want and why and focusing on how to get that is giving me all sorts of ideas and general food for thought. A strategy session is definitely something to consider.'

Andrew J

The environment

There is a lot of media speculation about house prices. The buzz at property network meetings is all about 'flipping' (see Chapter 10) and capital gain. I believe that listening to the masses without a clear understanding of how money works (see Chapter 3) could easily pave the way to financial ruin for many.

The speculation in the London market is clearly being driven by foreign investment. Property in London has become a valued and trusted asset class on the international markets. What about the rest of the UK? Very few foreign investors will see two-up two-downs in some town they have never heard of outside the M25 as an attractive investment for a capital strategy. So why would you?

In basic economic terms there needs to be a level of supply and demand in any market place. While there is a general shortage of property across England, outside of London have wages increased? Are the general population feeling more confident about the economy? Do they have massive savings stashed away?

The answer is no! In May 2014 I spoke at the Berkshire Property Meet to a couple of hundred investors. I explained the reality is that *asking* prices have definitely increased, fueled by some appauling estate agent practices like sealed bids and full and final offers. But are these properties being sold? With reports of more surveyors down-valuing properties[3] and the impact of the Mortgage Market Review (MMR), I am not convinced that sold prices are increasing that dramatically or will continue to rise in the long term.

Mortgage affordability, after the combined impact of the introduction of MMR and Chancellor George Osborne's 2014 Mansion House reforms of the Bank of England, means that new residential buyers will find mortgages harder to get and the loan to income ratios restricted.[4] *And* of course any borrowing must also be affordable at 7% interest. Therefore when considering buying to sell have you considered if your end user can borrow enough?

So how can they afford to borrow even more money from restrictive lenders to buy property increasing at 10% or more?

---

3   http://www.bbc.co.uk/news/business-27235170

4   http://www.bbc.co.uk/news/business-27813232

In 2013 I was interviewed by *The Guardian and Observer* and about gazumping. We placed a sensible offer on a property needing about £20,000 worth of work. Someone else offered over the asking price – why? No idea? The price paid was at the ceiling value of the street and with money spent on works that would bring the house to £20,000 over street value. There was no way to recoup that investment and having spent so much the return on the cash employed (equivalent to savings interest if the money had been left in the bank) was around 6%.

In spring 2014 we offered on a house and because of a sealed bid scenerio I decided to only offer the asking price £124,950. The other investor offered over £20,000 more. On a property worth only £124,500 – he is paying in excess of £145,000.

I have seen asking prices in one of my areas, in the north east of England, increase by £10,000 in the last six months. That's almost £20,000 per annum , over 20%! This is unsustainable and driven solely by mad cash-rich-investors. Yes buy in an area where there is tenant demand and a great return on investment (ROI), but stay calm, bid wisely and don't believe the capital dream. Be businesslike and check your spreadsheet – invest in cashflow and maybe be rewarded in the future with a capital gain, after years of financial freedom and peace of mind from the rental profit!

The changes in the mortgage markets over the last six years caught a lot of people off guard. That's why we need to understand the true worth of an investment – its return on investment (ROI). Let's get educated, and stay professional. Let's invest in property at a time when prices are lower than they have been for years. Let's capitalise on the great cashflows available and let's do it using other people's money wherever possible. However, let's do it using all of our business skills and understanding of the market, our service and of course the power of leverage.

Instead of seeing the purchase of a property costing very little of your own money as a good idea, a real business entrepreneur (something we need to be in order to be successful in property investing) would understand that you were taking on a debt that must be repaid with someone's money – if not the tenant's or another buyer's, then yours! The question to ask is 'What is the net cashflow?'

Section 1
Strategic Thinking:
The Business of
Investing

Chapter 1 The business of investing

During the last six years I have really come to appreciate how my change in mindset is crucial to my ongoing success in property and business. In 2008 I would have told you that I was a property investor. By 2012 I knew that I was a property business owner and not just because I was now running The Property Sourcers and The Sourcer's Apprentice, even within my own portfolio I understood that I was a property business owner.

More importantly I came to understand the value of my time. I know time is my most crucial resource. It is finite and irreplaceable. With the help of my personal metaphor 'The Property Mermaid', I can focus on my overall goal to to enjoy happiness, fun and adventures with my family and friends. Using my business experience and understanding I have been able to identify the most appropriate business and investment strategy to give me the cashflow I want, and the time to enjoy it.

In the following chapters I will explain each strategy in detail and explore the pros and cons in terms of time implications, cost to establish profit and lifestyle consequences. This will enable you to make better, more informed, decisions about which strategies will help you to achieve your goals more efficiently (notice I don't say more easily).

Before we start there are five concepts I want to explain:

1. Purpose, gratitude and focus – the why, how and what of a business mindset.
2. Personal financial equilibrium, financial security and don't give up your job.
3. The value of time – maximising results to enjoy more choice and happiness.
4. Strategic matching – free time, income needed and lifestyle.
5. Six steps to success.

1. In the beginning, there was the mind

- Why are some people more successful than others?
- Why are some people happy and others not?

The answers to the above are based on three aspects of the mind and how you choose to 'set' it: you might want to invest in property but for what purpose?

Successful people have a purpose. They generate income that will enable them to create a lifestyle of their design and choosing. What is your purpose? Instead of a passive approach, why not take action? Work out your income and expenses, ensure your lifestyle and income are in alignment – achieve a minimum of financial equilibrium (discussed on page 8). Then work towards creating the lifestyle of your choosing. Without this crucial piece of understanding you will struggle to implement the most efficient strategies to maximise on the property market.

The second aspect is gratitude; to be grateful for what you do have. You are among 10% of the richest people in the world by the fact that you live in the western world. It is easy in our consumer-led, materialistic and fast-paced lives to forget to really appreciate the finer things we have: love, friendship, a home and food to put on the table are just a few.

The third aspect is focus. When I learnt to focus I realised that I had the power to do anything I wanted, and of course with that came the responsibility for the outcome, I was both terrified and liberated. It meant that if I failed, it would be because of the decisions I made. But, equally, when I succeeded, then that would also be as a result of my decisions.

I choose to believe that we can do anything we put our minds to. This is a choice, an empowering one. Who do you feel has the power and control in your life? Now, if you are married, you might be tempted to say your partner. The reality is that we make decisions and those decisions give us our results. Some people make the decision to give the power and control of their lives to another person. Others struggle because they have not found the way to reclaim control of their lives. You can choose to believe that you can do anything if you put your mind to it, if you want. Equally, you could choose that nothing ever 'goes your way'.

As a direct result of this decision, you will feel powerful knowing that you can do anything. You will feel proud that you have achieved all that you have because you decided to take action. There was a time when my power was taken from me (notice the language – the power was outside of myself). I was disempowered, isolated and unable to see a way out. I was lost. Then I came to understand the importance of purpose, gratitude and focus. More importantly I made them my core values.

I will add one caveat. I totally acknowledge all the support I get. Without Bob, my love, my dive buddy and my business partner, at my side my life would be immeasurably harder. I know I can still achieve anything I want to, but it is so much nicer to have company on the journey. Without family, friends and colleagues my path to success would be longer, harder and much lonelier.

The compounding effect

The filters we use to sort through the information bombarding our brains, and our experiences in life, combine to shape how we view the world. Yet, you can literally re-programme your brain to think differently.

You must have heard of the saying 'It takes 21 days to create a habit'. It all just takes practise.

Jeff Olson, who wrote *The Slight Edge*, says that success principles start with taking one action every day that is on the path towards your goals. Every day we are faced with choices and, if we make the right choice, we get one step closer to that goal.

You may not realise until years down the line how each simple activity contributed, compounded and grew until success was inevitable. Make the wrong choice and it could be years before you realise the error of your ways and the opportunity you have lost.

I have already mentioned the importance of financial intelligence; understanding the power of leverage is crucial. Do you know that if you take £1 and double it the next day, then double it again the next day, you will have over £1 million in 21 days?

Look at the table below. It's 11 days before you get to over £1,000, and 15 days before you get to over £16,000. Then, in the last six days, compounding takes the money to over £1 million.

It can be hard to see the benefits of small actions in the early days, one pound at a time, but what about if you know the benefits are multiplying every minute?

Day 1	1	Day 8	128	Day 15	16,384
Day 2	2	Day 9	256	Day 16	32,768
Day 3	4	Day 10	512	Day 17	65,536
Day 4	8	Day 11	1,024	Day 18	131,072
Day 5	16	Day 12	2,048	Day 19	262,144
Day 6	32	Day 13	4,096	Day 20	524,288
Day 7	64	Day 14	8,192	Day 21	1,048,576

Table 1: The powerful effect of compounding

Now compare this table to the second example and table opposite:

What if you took your coffee and applied the same concept? Know that every time you buy a latté or an espresso shot, every time you spend that pound it is lost, it can never be multiplied by you again – it is now multiplying for someone else.

Do I need to go on?

Year	Annum	Lost opportunity
1	-660	660
2	-1,320	1,320
3	-1,980	2,640
4	-2,640	5,280
5	-3,300	10,560
6	-3,960	21,120
7	-4,620	42,240
8	-5,280	84,480
9	-5,940	168,960
10	-6,600	337,920
11	-7,260	675,840
12	-7,920	1,351,680
13	-8,580	Do I need to go on?

Table 2: Assume 5 days x £2.75 x 48 weeks = £660 per annum

In the first column you cumulatively lose the cash you are spending. In the second column you cumulatively lose the opportunity to double your money. That is over 1,351,680 lost opportunities to grow your money from negative compounding – all because you bought a coffee or gave your money away before you made it work for you. Please don't interpret this as being against charitable donations – absolutely we need to give back – but build your capital first and then you can give so much more.

If there is one thing that we all hear time and time again, it's all about having the 'right mindset'. Some people dismiss personal development and neurolinguistic programming (NLP) as being a bit 'spooky'. Others think they are fine, and a small number embrace the concepts and become really successful.

Actually, everyone will be successful eventually, the question is how successful? And how long will it take you to get there? Could you be more efficient, more grateful, and more focused?

2. Personal financial equilibrium – the path to path security

Personal financial equilibrium is the foundation from which all future family wealth can be built. Personal financial equilibrium means that you have at least as much income (if not more) coming into your bank account as you do costs, bills and direct debits leaving it.

In the last three years I have worked with hundreds of people and I always start by asking them whether they have personal financial equilibrium.

So many clients do not track their personal income and expenses. They might worry about bills but that is not helpful and not productive. When I first looked at my own personal financial equilibrium I saved £455 per calendar month by reviewing my insurance policies, subscriptions and general spending habits. If you don't already have a spreadsheet, please feel free to download a copy of the one I use with clients here http://vickiwusche.co.uk/blog/pfe/

The Challenge:

1. Complete estimates of your monthly outgoings – without referring to your statements or receipts. Note how much you think you spend.

2. Monitor your income accurately over the next month (just start now and do it for four weeks).

3. Identify the financial myths you were telling yourself.

4. Take action to bring your cashflow into alignment to create your personal financial equilibrium and then grow your income from there.

I firmly hold the belief that it is irresponsible and dangerous to take on massive debt (which comes with most mortgages) in order to invest in property if you do not completely understand your own personal financial circumstances.

Understand money and the value of it – this is a critical factor in your property business and its success. We have all heard about the lottery winners who lose everything and more within years of their big wins. Why does this happen? You need to have a wealthy mindset and the right knowledge of how to invest, protect and leverage your money.

Once you understand your personal financial equilibrium you can create a business goal to earn for example £2,500 per month from property, so that you have enough income to cover your expenses.

Do not rush to give up your day job as so many speakers and trainers encourage. Wait until you have at least double your expenses in income if not triple. Wait until you can prove to a mortgage lender that you are a safe person to take out a mortgage. Many people, in the rush (and the hype) to give up work and claim that goal, find themselves unable to secure lending from banks! Be sensible – be strategic.

With £5,000 income from property you will definitely feel more financially secure. This will enable you to think even more clearly and strategically about your next goal. By the time you earn triple your expenses in income from property you will have enough recurring income to enable you to make new decisions about your lifestyle, maybe where you choose to live and how you choose to use your time.

3. Value your time – it's irreplaceable

It was the untimely death of my best friend Sally that really made me question how I used my time. I started to recognise activities I did out of habit or a desire to help others. These activities were not helping or supporting me in the achievement of my own personal and business goals.

I identified business activities that did not give a decent return on my time (e.g. network marketing). The first step was to calculate the value of my time and then use that formula to logically evaluate which activities would help me achieve my financial goals more quickly.

For example to earn a starting figure of £60,000 per annum, as a business owner and solo-preneur I had to be responsible for many areas of my business: accounts, administration, business development, looking for business (income speculation), actual income generation and of course leave room for some fun.

I cover this concept in depth in *Make More Money from Property: From investor thinking to a business mindset* (p51–54).

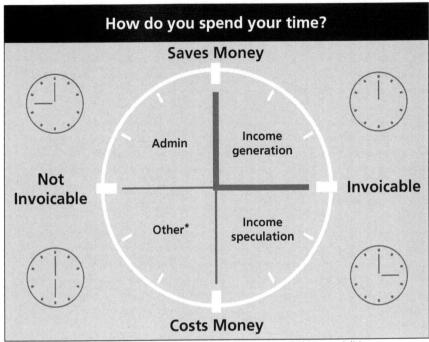

How do you spend your time?

Saves Money

Admin

Income generation

Not Invoicable

Invoicable

Other*

Income speculation

Costs Money

Other – non-business activities, e.g. personal development, sports, hobbies, socialising.

To make the maths easier I decided to not work weekends and to only work for ten months a year. Apart from the obvious correlation with The Property Mermaid metaphor and my love of holidays, no matter how hard you might want to work others will take breaks at Christmas, Easter and other times of the year. So it is better to be realistic about the time you can work and earn money.

So when you do the calculation allow one day per week for each of the admin, business development and income speculating roles. That leaves two days per week for pure income generation (and the weekends for fun).

In a seven hour day, working two days per week and ten months per year you will have a total of 560 hours in which to earn £60,000 (the target example above). That's approximately £107.14 per hour. Now double this figure to allow for tax, national insurance, petrol, phone bills and other basic business costs. These will be different for everyone and vary from strategy to strategy – I am simply showing you a process – something to help set your mind.

Again to make the maths nice and easy let's just assume, after doubling, your gross hourly rate is £200. Now you have a tool to evaluate your activities.

Lots of people say the television is a time sucker and the Devil's work. Maybe a lot of it is. However if I have worked hard during the day, focused on my goals and earned my targets then I enjoy chilling out in the evening with family watching a film or comedy programme – that is worth £200 per hour to me. Even though the example above was based on a weekly hourly rate, I like to still use this number during my social life and non-working time. It creates a great habit and helps me evaluate how I use all my time wisely, and for a conscious purpose, rather than waste it.

If you are watching TV during the day and have more bills than income then maybe you can see why.

When you go on a course, attend an event – especially if you do this a lot then factor in the cost of your time as well as the fee to attend and then evaluate how you will earn that money back. If you are not sure then maybe you need to rethink your reason for attending. What is the return on your time worth.

4. Strategic matching – have the time, money and lifestyle

This concept enables you to recognise the emotive draw of another person's success and to analyse its relevance to you.

I regularly hear property investors speak about their strategies. Some are clearly selling a course, others are telling their story and adding value for the audience. But what do you want to achieve? If you read your life story in the future, how would you want to write now? What is the best strategy for you and how can you choose it?

This third edition of *Using Other People's Money* will help you to compare the demands of each strategy as well as the time and money needed to implement them and become successful until the point of income. By the end of the chapter you will understand the realistic income potential of each strategy and the impact on your lifestyle to achieve that level of success.

This concept of strategically matching your personal goals to what are in effect a series of techniques of investing, will help you clearly align your goals and outcomes. That has to have an impact on your success and your mindset, so creating greater success and a better, happier lifestyle. Each investment technique will be analysed as we progress through the chapters, using your hourly rate (what your time is worth) and a realistic expectation of the strategy, and an awareness of the time commitment needed to bring the strategy into being.

5. Six steps to success

Whether you choose to see what you are doing as sourcing and creating a property business (the premise of *Make More Money from Property: From investor thinking to a business mindset*) or you just decide to invest in property for yourself, there are six steps to success:

1. Why? Your purpose – what is your version of The Property Mermaid metaphor?

2. What? Your model – using strategic matching of techniques.

3. Where? Your area – as influenced by time and technique.

4. Who? Your investment client, your tenant, seller or your buyer.

5. When? Time practicalities – how much can you afford?

6. How? The systems – to ensure you can do it again and again.

Make More Money from Property: From investor thinking to a business mindset explains in more detail about how money works, leverage, hourly rates and the business of investing and developing systems.

Chapter 2 Strategic investing: how to become a business owner

How to apply strategic investing to your portfolio

Instead of being a property investor who buys houses and gets stuck when there is no more money, I believe that if you think like and become a property business owner with all the concepts talked about so far, then you will grow your business and your portfolio quicker and more easily than many others.

There are two selling points for me:

1. You can start thinking in terms of products and services and that is more creative than just houses.

2. You can start to leverage your time and money and, more importantly, other people's time and money, and all by strategically matching your investment technique with your desired financial outcome and lifestyle.

Think about products and services for a minute – how is this different from thinking about houses? I recognised that my tenant was actually a customer who I was selling to. I was selling them the idea that they wanted to live in my property and that they wanted to stay there for a long time. Then I thought about the seller of a property I wanted to buy – what service could I offer them? Then my estate agent and so on. It has changed the way I do business and has opened up lots of opportunities that I have put into practice.

I also thought about what I had to offer – what do people who I meet want from me? In January 2010, I spoke at the two January Berkshire Property Meetings for just five to seven minutes. Afterwards, I was surrounded by people asking questions and I soon realised that people wanted to know what I had been doing. So I wrote a book. I saw the book as a way to use my time effectively – write once, share many times. Now I had my first product.

This time I have written a book using a better more professional, cost-effective and time-effective system. This book will generate more profit than the first book because I have employed a great team, the strategy was planned from the start and the marketing is better – I recognise this is a product. The fourth book will do even better as I apply the new lessons I am learning and so on.

The books are products for sale – I would just like to add that you don't get rich from writing books unless they include the attraction of a certain Mr Grey! But what a book does offer is credibility, marketing, PR opportunities, a way for people to start to get to know you. I regularly have clients get in touch, practically presold to the idea of working with me either as a mentee or a sourcing client because by reading my books they feel they know me and know what I do.

Finally, in 2011, I took the very challenging step (for me as a committed control freak) to outsource some of my business. Even as I write, I can think of more tasks that I want to hand over to my team. I initially used a virtual PA who worked part time in my business to help me by doing the routine and repeatable jobs. Now the business has grown I have one full-time member of staff, two business partners, a new apprentice, a part-time book keeper handling the accounts, marketing and PR for two days per month and of course the all-important cleaner. Plus there are the professional team of brokers, solicitors, tax advisors and builders.

Being an old-fashioned and unnecessary control freak is something that has definitely slowed me down as I hold a limiting belief that I have to meet people who work with me. Hence, virtual 'anythings' are a challenge! Having said this, I know plenty of investors who are landlords because they don't trust a letting agent! I am now in the process of creating a replicable system that other investors can follow – complete with 'how to' and 'what if' instructions – another new product.

So, why be a business owner? Because you can leverage other people's time and money to grow your property portfolio more quickly and more easily. Why do that? So that you can be financially secure and start enjoying the financial freedom and lifestyle that you want.

Is this compelling enough?

How do you become a business owner?

You need to take this new way of understanding property investment and apply it to your own circumstances. You need to decide on your own repeatable and replicable model of property sourcing. You need to identify where your skills and experience lie, what your knowledge and passion is about. This will form the basis of your business model.

So just to repeat the steps:

1. Know why you want to invest in property. What do you expect to get out of it? What will the business look like? How much will you earn (do the maths)? How will you earn your cashflow?

2. Get financially educated; you have started by reading this book, now read Kiyosaki if you haven't already, and not just *Rich Dad, Poor Dad*. *Read Rich Dad's Conspiracy of the Rich: The 8 New Rules of Money* and *An Unfair Advantage: The Power of Financial Education*. Look at who you mix with and what groups you attend. Expand your network. Join a business networking group, one that does not burden you with building other people's businesses like the BRN (Business Referral Network) or BNI (Business Network International). Have conversations with your accountant, tax advisor and other business owners. Get a good broker who follows the market and can discuss the mood of the Monetary Policy Committee with you – we all know interest rates will rise. Who can you connect with, talk to and listen to about all things financial and economic? Stay connected with us and listen to our webinars – get our free newsletters!

3. Pick the right strategy and know the other strategies that can be used if need be. Remember about the value of your time – make sure the strategy will pay you a decent 'wage' for your time, otherwise Tesco, Marks & Spencer or Boots start to look like a better option! Understand what you want to achieve financially and then give yourself the best possible chance of achieving it. My money 'is on' and comes from property sourcing. I am my own client and so my system is replicable. It is costed to make sure I earn a decent amount for my time (which is a valuable and limited resource – the only limited resource in reality!).

4. Leverage where possible – use other people's money and other people's time. You will need to understand the relative cost of money and return on investment in order to explain the opportunity to potential clients. Outsource by using a letting agent, bookkeeper, accountant, builder and, if you can, a cleaner. Work these costings into your business model.

5. Understand what you have to offer your clients. What is your service? Why should they sell to you or buy or rent from you and not someone else? To do this you will need to understand what you know, what you have experience of, what your skills are and where your passion lies. It is one of the fundamental bits of personal analysis that I do with a new mentee, because if you can't explain to me why I should do business with you, then I will work with someone else who can.

6. Then remember in this seemingly 'me-me' world that what you have to offer has to be all about 'them' and not about 'you'. Making that transition from understanding yourself to understanding your client market is crucial; so crucial that the success of your business will rest upon you achieving it. Know your client, picture them, know where to find them and always speak directly to them. Refine your understanding of your client market over time – it will change. What you have to offer your client has to be good, but it does not have to be perfect first time! Develop your niche and tailor your message accordingly.

7. Know your value. What are you selling and what is it worth? Recognise whether you are selling a replicable model (what you do) or the skills to act as an agent (not location or strategy specific).

8. Get the right team. I have already mentioned that you need to speak to the right people to increase your financial knowledge; you also need the right team to deliver a service to your clients. Know that you can trust the people you are building your business around. You don't need to use just one solicitor or even just one broker. A level of consistency will build trust and relationships, but you need to be prepared to change if their ability to meet your service needs doesn't come up to your expected standard or response times. Just a word of caution here – if you are only passing on one deal a quarter, you are probably not a top client – so build on your business and that relationship first. How much business you do with another business will reflect in how much they value you or even remember you.

In *Make More Money from Property: From investor thinking to a business mindset* I explain the practicalities and specifics of setting up a sourcing business and, of course, you can access the free webinars, videos and audios that accompany this book on TheSourcersApprentice.com

Section 2
The Business of Funding

Chapter 3 The new rules of money

You might wonder when we are going to get to the techniques of using other people's money; how to invest in property. Well, this is all part of it.

If you don't know how your mind works (Chapter 1) and you don't know how to invest strategically (Chapter 2), then the money you borrow as a result of the techniques discussed later in this book will not create you financial freedom – they may well lead to your financial ruin.

This is neither a game nor a hobby. This is a serious and seriously fun business to be in: exciting and challenging, rewarding and frustrating, but above all wealth creating if you do it right.

One of the key things about investing in property or using other people's money is to really understand how money works – to have a high level of 'financial intelligence'. To know the meaning of the terms asset and liability, good debt, bad debt, to understand your financial statement and your level of 'credit-ability' or credibility.

The current dis-education system

It is a real shame we are not taught more about money in school or how to use credit properly or what it means. We are all taught to get a job and then buy our home with a mortgage – living happily ever after until the mortgage is paid off in time for us to retire. What the system does not allow for is an insufficient pension, people living longer and being healthier. What do you want your retirement to be like?

I intend to live life to the maximum and I don't want to have to sell my home in order to stay warm and fed. So I choose to do something about it now!

The government has been sending out the wrong message to young people for years, encouraging them to take up student loans and that it's 'OK' to have loans, go to university and end up in massive debt.

All these young people will leave university with £5,000–£20,000 worth of debt. On top of this, when they leave university, they will get a job, meet a partner and, at some point, want to buy a house. However, they will already be saddled with debt before they even consider a mortgage, and with no understanding about how much money it's costing them. Just like we were.

Having said this, if it weren't for 'debt' and the people higher up the money chain making the money from the people lower down the chain through the interest payments, the economy wouldn't be working at all. Our economy is fuelled by debt, by the lending and borrowing of money. The financial sector is one of our major industries.

It is important to understand that there is good debt and bad debt, and everybody should learn the difference. Unfortunately, it's so easy to get bad debt and end up paying four times the ticket price for a seemingly cheap item or paying for the next 20 years.

Good debt vs. bad debt

Good debt is what we use when we invest in property and other 'incoming-generating assets'. An income-generating asset is something that puts money into your pocket even when you don't work.

Good debt is what we use to buy an asset that gives us income in our pockets. We can go on to use the surplus from the rent (money left after the mortgage and house costs are paid) to buy other things, to pay our living costs, so it's using debt in a good way to produce cashflow coming into our pockets.

Bad debt would be something like a loan that you take out to buy a car. You can't earn any money from the car (unless you are a taxi driver). A car immediately loses value, plus there are costs for maintenance. It takes money out of your pocket.

Another example of bad debt is using a credit card to buy a holiday or clothes. If you do not clear the credit card at the end of the month, you will pay interest on the outstanding balance. The interest rates vary, but a holiday for two costing £1,500 at an interest rate of 28% is costing you nearly £35 a month extra.

While the concepts of good debt and bad debt have been explained, it is also important to understand the terms: asset and liability. An asset, like good debt, puts money into your pocket. A liability, by definition, is something that takes money out of your pocket even when you do work. When we take out a buy-to-let or investment mortgage we are borrowing money from the bank, we are using that debt to buy an asset. We have a tenant who pays for the interest on that debt.

Some people think an example of an asset is the house that they live in, but this is not an asset. As with the example of using a loan to buy a car, your home is not an asset because the mortgage payments are made out of your pocket. The repairs, the bills, the furnishings are all costs to you. Your home is not an asset because it takes money out of your pocket; some people find this explanation a shock!

Build your skills, build a business and build your cashflow

Lots of property investors and entrepreneurs have second businesses. You need to choose carefully and do your research. Think about where your interests lie – do you want to deal with products or services? I recommend that you consider setting up your own property-related business.

As I mentioned before one of my businesses is called The Sourcer's Apprentice; I chose to create a property training business because of my background skills as a teacher and my desire to share my knowledge. I also run a property sourcing business called The Property Sourcers, which enables me to focus on sourcing deals and maintaining my contacts and relationships, so I am always ready to buy a property when a good opportunity comes along.

Why did I set up more businesses – where is my focus? I identified firstly that I was bored not working; financial freedom is a great aspiration but then you need to do something with your time. Then, secondly, I realised that I needed to enhance and improve my ability to sell, which is a vital skill. I also wanted to build a business that enabled me to leverage the time of others so I could earn while I was not working. A long-term retirement plan for when I really was ready to give up and do nothing!

Property enables me to leverage my money and business enables me to leverage my time and that of my team/business partners.

So what about focus? Well in the past I have had multi-level marketing (MLM) businesses (two in fact) and I found that they distracted me as they were not about property – I believe focus is crucial. If you know how to do something, why not monetise that activity? I have a 'story' that enables me to create a link and focus between my businesses – a pitch if you like.

> I help people understand how they can make more money from property, initially helping them identify unrealised financial resources and create their own personal investment plan (my strategy sessions) so they can create a cashflowing property portfolio. Some clients

have busy lives and they simply want me to source a property portfolio for them (sourcing services). Other clients want to learn how to do it themselves, so I have a training business and teaching resources that make it easy for them to learn how to create a cashflowing business (mentoring, online courses and books).

This story about my businesses (or pitch) which I can use to explain what I do to others, enables me to remember how all the pieces fit together and to maintain my focus, which is either buying houses (for me or for clients) or teaching people how to buy houses (a three second version of the same pitch). There is no distraction – well except writing books and holidays – but I enjoy that.

I recommend developing your business skills; I highly recommend focusing on your goal. If you are not ready to create your own business yet, then be single minded in identifying a business that will expose you to new situations or enable you to develop new skills, like selling, or negotiating, working on the phone or speaking to strangers. Wherever there is a gap in your business skills, fill it or find a partner that can.

Your financial statement – what is it and what does it mean?

It is definitely *not* about your bank statement and how much money you put into the bank or take out. A financial statement shows your assets, your liabilities, your income and expenses. Once you have mapped out all of this, you can see the state of your finances – in a sense your financial position. I introduced the concept of personal financial equilibrium in Chapter 1. The financial statement expands this tool to include assets and liabilities.

Some people may have bought assets that don't actually cashflow, or they may have a negative cashflow across the whole portfolio that could be solved by repurposing or selling just one property.

If you build up your own assets to become cashflowing then you can become financially self-sufficient when you are older. You can still collect your pension if there is one, but you won't be reliant on it. That is my plan!

Unfortunately, with the devaluation of money in real terms, your savings won't buy you much in 20 years. However, income-generating assets will increase in value and rise in line with inflation. When you understand how the money flows and the real value of the assets that you own, then you will be in a strong position for the future.

Are you living above your means? You really need to understand your financial statement if you are going to be really financially successful.

History of money and why it's not worth anything now

Historically, the way money is viewed, used and valued has changed dramatically. It was switched from the 'Gold Standard' back in 1971. Until the 1970s, the value of the US dollar was linked to gold assets held in reserve (the Federal Reserve). In other words, you could exchange your dollar for gold. This system was removed in the 1970s and now money has simply become an exchange of debt note.

It also means that a government can now print money when it decides, because it does not need the gold to back up that debt note. We have already seen the British government print extra money as part of the quantitative easing program. If there are more pound notes in circulation, then the value of each note effectively decreases and inflation becomes a real danger.

As the economy shifts and changes in the new global market, trading in bonds (debt notes) could see countries reach the edge of bankruptcy again and again due to market speculation – that's not a good place to be.

Controlling assets – taking the first step

You have far more control over an asset than you have over money in the bank. With an asset like property, you can buy it at a discount and add value by renovating or adding rooms.

You can manage your income by managing your tenant, who ultimately provides the cash through rental payments. In reality, your tenant is also your asset, not just the bricks and mortar.

The property investment journey starts with understanding and getting educated first. Do things the right way; don't expose yourself to any uncalculated risks by not having the right information.

- Start slowly and it won't be long before you never look back.
- Take those first small steps and change things.
- Don't ever just take one person's word; listen to a number of people.

As I mentioned before, Jeff Olson, the author of the book *The Slight Edge*, states that every day we have the choice to make the right decision and, if we make that right decision day after day, it's not long before the benefits of our decisions and actions create exponential growth.

Cashflow – Monopoly on steroids

Along side selling, understanding your belief and attitude about money and business, developing your skill with money is crucial. In order to help you understand more about money and how it works, I highly recommend you play Kiyosaki's board game called Cashflow.

The game can be played in groups at organised Cashflow Clubs across the UK, which are designed to teach and help you to play the game with others. It is well known that if you practise what you are learning, you retain the information better. A good place to find your nearest official Cashflow Club is at: www.meetup.com/

Or you can just buy the game for yourself and play it with your family and friends. There are valuable lessons to be learned.

Chapter 4 Money, debt, leverage and keeping score

For many people money is an emotional response to family 'stories' or inter-generational myths. Did your grandparents or parents ever tell you that 'money doesn't grow on trees'. While true, in fact, they were actually sharing their belief that money is not abundant.

The reality is that there are trillions of pounds in our global economy. Money, usually in the form of paper or metallic tokens, represents an exchange. Some people exchange their time for a trinket, experience or a fundamental basic of life, like food, heat or shelter.

In the last chapter I discussed the difference between good debt and bad debt – a critical key distinction in building your family wealth. Money is also a resource. That is how I choose to experience it. I recognise that it is finite but that it can be leveraged. As I demonstrated in the tables in Chapter 1, understanding that leverage is a powerful technique to develop your family wealth will make the next few years much easier.

A property example would be:

Spend £100,000 on a single property bought outright for cash and you could receive £500 per month rent and that would be profit (putting to one side buying costs, letting agent fees and insurance to make the example easier).

Use the £100,000 to pay for four 25% deposits on four houses. Now you have four times £500 rent coming in. After paying the mortgage at £312.50 (£75,000 at 5% interest) you would have £187.50 profit per house.

That's a total of £750 cash per month made by investing the same £100,000 in a different way – using leverage.

When you combine an understanding of money as a resource, a tool to be used via leverage, with an understanding of the implications of good and bad debt, you have the foundations for great investment decisions.

I suppose I then have to ask why some investors continually seek to remortgage properties, to pull their cash out to buy second, third and fourth properties, when the process of remortgaging reduces the cashflow and increases the debt and the risk of exposure when interest rates rise.

If we take our four properties from the example above and remortgage them to release the £100,000 again, each individual house would then have a mortgage of £100,000 and a mortgage cost of £416.66, that leaves a profit of just £83 per property; just £333 instead of £750.

Okay you would be looking to buy another four properties (let's keep everything simply and the same to explain a point):

The four new properties could bring in £750 giving you eight properties with a total profit of £1,083. What if interest rates rose to 6%? How would you cope?

Four properties with borrowing of £100,000 @ 6% is a monthly mortgage cost of £500 – no profit.

Four new properties with borrowing of £75,000 @ 6% is a monthly mortgage cost of £375.

Giving a total profit for eight properties of just £500.

When interest rates rise to 7% the eight properties would cost you £4,083.32 per month in mortgage payments alone! Your total rent is £4,000. While only minus £83.32 per month. What if a boiler breaks down? How are you sleeping now?

If you had kept just the first four houses and the same £75,000 mortgage you would still have £250 profit per month – not ideal but it is still positive cashflow and there is equity in the houses.

This is the time to be cautious. Consider the example above, just a 2% rise in interest rates and you are broke. Have you got property now? Have you stress tested your portfolio? Do you know what impact a 1% interest rate rise will have – what about a 3% rise? Also, consider that the new MMR is testing the affordability of residential buyers at 7%. Why, what do they do now? Do the powers that be believe that interest rates might rise to 7%?

The affordability criteria only applies to the residential market because they don't care if your buy-to-let portfolio becomes repossessed, but I am guessing you would care!

There is an election due and I think that will have an influence (no matter what politicians say) on interest rates and when we will see them rise. If the economy does start to show signs of significant growth then the Bank of England will need to increase interest rates, that could happen in 2015 – although I think later in the year as no government wants interest rates to rise just before an election. While savers would be happy, the impact on business and home owners could be significant. Leave it too long and more people may get carried away with their debt fuelled spending habits and then the interest rate rise will be even worse!

There are three golden rules to making money from property investment and this book focuses on techniques to access and leverage money to invest in property:

1. Understand money, debt and leverage.

2. Understand the consequences and risk of each investment decision.

3. Consider each investment technique in light of your personal strategic goals – it's not a race!

Buying with credit cards – tread carefully

There are property investment courses that encourage students to manipulate their credit cards to increase their credit limits and negotiate 0% credit card facilities. They do this to show the students how easy it is and to demonstrate that you can negotiate. But credit cards have consequences for your credit report and credit scores so you need to tread carefully.

Having said that understanding how to use credit cards (or any form of bank lending) to your own advantage is vital if you are to make the best use of your investment capital and cashflow. Credit cards and the companies that run them are notorious for charging high rates of interest on any outstanding balances.

Many of you will already have credit cards and use them regularly. A surprising number of you will still hold the old view that credit cards are 'bad'. My aim is to explain how you can use credit cards to your advantage, avoid high interest charges and pitfalls, and increase your investment capital.

I thought you said credit cards were bad?

Let's start with dispelling the myth that credit cards are bad news. What makes them 'good' or 'bad' is how you use them. For example, going on a 'shopping spree', whether it's clothes, electronics or holidays, and not clearing the outstanding balance on your statement in full is not only bad it is mad. To explain briefly, this is because the outstanding balance will accrue interest at the high rate that your card company charges, often in excess of 29%. Therefore, any savings made at the point of purchase is not only wiped out but actually exceeded by the ongoing monthly costs charged by the company. I will come to some more examples later on.

So, if you use credit cards to buy frivolous items or 'stuff' that does not ultimately return an income, then, yes, they are bad news. Credit cards teach you to spend money you don't have without a thought for clearing the debt.

However, in its simplest form, a credit card, if used properly, can give you up to 45 days extra money – interest free.

Let me just explain that last sentence. Immediately after you receive your last credit card statement and demand for payment, you could buy products or services using the 'credit' available on your credit card. Then you would have use of that money/credit for approximately 45 days or longer until your next credit card statement and demand for payment arrives in the post. This is using a credit card for maximum gain, your gain. By buying products like building materials or paying for surveys on your credit card, you can effectively keep your actual cash in your bank account for a further 45 days.

This section will discuss some of the facts, tips and information 'not widely' known about credit cards, credit rating and how to protect your score while getting the maximum possible out of the banks.

What the bank wants

Banks want you to stay ignorant of the game and how it works. They want you to take out credit cards and buy stuff that really you can't afford, so that at the end of the month you don't clear your credit card balance and instead pay them an extortionate rate of interest.

On the other hand, they now also want you to be the model and perfect borrower. From a secured lending perspective, the underwriters of mortgages want you to demonstrate that you know how to manage your money. The way that you do this is to limit the amount of unsecured borrowing (credit cards) that you have available. Do not apply for too many credit cards and do not 'max out' your credit cards, using every last pound available to you, as you will look out of control. And, of course, pay back your cards regularly and even overpay them now and then. Let's take all of these points in turn.

Limit the number of cards that you have

Let's start with the situation that you already have credit cards.

At this point, I would suggest that you review all of your cards, how you use them, how you clear the balances and, of course, check your credit rating. If you have a good score, and we discuss this in more detail on page 31, then leave things alone.

Alternatively, if you have a lot of cards and a poor score, it could imply that you are not managing your cards well – we discuss some good habits for managing your cards on page 34.

You may be one of a surprisingly large number of people that either do not have a credit card or have only one or two in their name. This is perfectly fine and please do not rush out and apply for another six cards! The same principles apply to you as everyone else. Think about how you currently use your cards and how you clear them.

Check your credit rating and if you have a very good score and you are not just about to apply for a mortgage, then you might want to consider applying for a new credit card – especially if there is a 0% offer available.

However, there is no point getting a 0% offer if you do not have a specific business reason and use for the money.

Do not apply for too many

I just mentioned applying for a new card and now I am saying don't apply for too many. Of course you can apply for a new credit card, but I would suggest that you have a specific reason or use for applying for it. Only apply for a credit card if you have checked that your credit report and credit score are in good order. And definitely, in my opinion, do not apply for a credit card just before you want to apply for a mortgage, as the credit card company will conduct a credit search on you and this will be recorded on your credit report. It may not count against you, but do you want to take the risk? Think about your actions and plan carefully.

It is good practice to have one or two cards that you use to purchase goods (shopping or petrol) on a regular basis, and then pay them off in full every month. You might also have one or two cards that you use for 'business' purposes, such as paying surveyor or broker fees. Again, clearing the card monthly.

You may also have borrowed money on a 0% credit card to fund the cost of materials for a refurbishment project, like a new kitchen or plumbing materials, then you would be making only minimum payments. Imagine looking at your credit report through the eyes of an underwriter who is considering lending you a lot of money on a mortgage. This sort of behaviour might look like someone who knew how to manage their finances.

Alternatively, if as an underwriter you saw a credit report that had a number of applications for credit cards one month and then more the next month, you might consider that this person was desperate to get hold of credit and that they may be out of control or a high risk.

Don't 'max out' your credit limit

This is very similar in principle to the point about the number of cards you have. Credit reports record the activity on your credit card – this is explained further on the next page. Imagine you are an underwriter considering whether or not to approve a loan. Which person would you think was a better risk: the person who had a number of cards all with maximum borrowing that were not cleared monthly, or the person who had a number of cards, some cleared in full and others with a modest outstanding balance?

It is good practice to make sure that you do not over use every last bit of credit available on your card, while at the same time making sure that you use up to the limit and clear it regularly. This may sound confusing but think of it this way: be very aware of your credit limit and on certain cards work carefully to spend close to your limit by the end of the monthly period and then clear down the balance. This way you are showing the card lender that you need that amount of credit limit and you can manage your financial affairs carefully. However do not use all your cards to the very limit all the time without clearing them regularly as, again, you may look desperate for cash.

Pay back regularly and even overpay

It is absolutely vital that you set up a direct debit on all cards and, in fact, all loans that you take out. Make sure that you know exactly how much available cash you need in your bank account to pay the minimum payments. By using direct debits you avoid the fatal error of missing a payment.

Missed payments are, in the eyes of underwriters, the sign of a careless borrower or someone whose borrowing is out of control. Even a missed payment on a mobile phone contract is carelessness. Your credit score will be affected and most mortgage lenders will refuse to lend to you if you demonstrate this behaviour.

It can be good practice to occasionally overpay on your cards. If you have a 0% card offer, then set up a direct debit and each month make an extra payment to show that you can afford to clear the debt. If you are using a card for regular monthly expenses, then each month you will know that the amount outstanding on the card, and due for payment, is actually more in real terms as you will have continued to spend. So make the occasional overpayment. If the statement states that you owe £500 and you know in real terms it is closer to £600, then pay more than the £500 to show that you can.

How can you use credit cards to your advantage?

Credit cards, if used properly, can fund the refurbishment of properties, as mentioned above, or fund the deposits to buy new properties. They are simply another means of getting money for nothing, or very cheaply if you do it right.

They are a relatively easy and, of course, unsecured way to access additional money. However, like all things involving money, interest payments and time limits, they only work if you know what you are doing. Let's get into the detail and discuss credit scores.

The do's and don'ts of credit cards and your credit score

Your credit score needs to be managed carefully. Contact the three credit reference agencies, Equifax and Experian are more popular but also check Callcredit and look at your credit score.

Search for the Which Credit Report 2011 or check out their website.[5]

You should be aiming for a good or excellent score. Make sure that all the information they hold about you is correct and rectify any information that is incorrect or missing, so that your credit record is accurate. You might ask, why contact all the agencies? This is because different lenders use different companies, and the companies themselves hold slightly different information on you. Experian hold approximately one year of detailed information on you. So, as long as you do not miss payments or over apply for cards, you will likely have a good score.

Let's just re-emphasise the following as I believe this is the foundation to using your credit cards expertly:

- Do not miss a payment – it is vital that every single credit card that you have is set up with a minimum direct debit in place. If anything happens, such as a postal strike or holiday, then you know your payments will always be made.
- Don't over apply for cards – there is a temptation to apply for lots of cards once you learn the system. Don't! It will significantly reduce your credit score. Why? Because one of the 'markers' or factors that lenders look at is how many loan or credit applications you have made.

Credit scores are a system used by credit rating agencies to give you a numerical value based on the risk you pose to lenders. The higher the score (top score 999), the better potential client you are. The lower the score, the worse risk you present to a lender. The risk is whether you will default on your payments. It is not only the debt you take on and how you manage it that counts. Your voter registration needs to show your residential history – gaps need to be explained. As young people are so mobile these days it's vital to ensure that voters registration, and bills follow you from house to house. You will need to provide proof of identity to get a loan and you will need utility bills in your name at your residential address to confirm that.

I have a client – very wealthy and cash rich – whose credit history is immaculate. After taking six months off to go travelling they now cannot get a loan because there is a period where some bills went to a family member's address, others stayed on the old house as they could be accessed online, and the investor was not registered to vote anywhere as they were travelling. Be organised and sadly in this case follow the rules. The credit agencies big

---

5 http://www.which.co.uk/money/credit-cards-and-loans/guides/your-credit-report-explained/checking-your-credit-report/

brother and the lenders want to know where you have been, and what debt you have. Be precise.

Why is it so important to understand about credit reports and how the companies work? Well, lenders have to lend a certain amount of money each month (they have budget or target figures). Once they reach this target (or get close to it), they will start to get choosier about who they lend money to and will raise the minimum credit score limit. So, in the first few weeks of a month (and again on a quarterly basis), lenders may offer mortgages to people with scores as low as 800 (a good rating normally), but then suddenly anything less that 999 would be rejected as not good enough.

Also, you may have no problem getting loans from Birmingham Midshires (BMS), and then suddenly be refused by The Mortgage Works (TMW) because they use a different credit agency. As more mortgage products start to come to the market, it is highly likely that they will only offer the more advantageous products to the better clients with the best credit reports and scores – and you want that to be you.

How do banks score?

Your own bank will score you differently as it can see what you spend on a daily basis. The bank understands how your money goes in and out of your account. Of course, the bank likes to see that you are paying in more money than you are withdrawing on a monthly basis. They have a more intimate knowledge of you, especially if you have been a client for years and have a number of accounts. Alternatively, you may find your high street bank is not offering products that are favourable to you as a prospective property investor. You will need to discuss commercial lending on a business basis and that is another whole chapter in its own right.

What is gearing?

Gearing is when a lender looks at how much you have actually borrowed, particularly on unsecured lending like credit cards, against how much available credit you have. You need to get to a position where you are borrowing under 50% of your potential borrowing – i.e. have a gearing ratio of less than 50%. How do you work this out? Add up the total debt on all your credit cards and divide it by the total of all your credit limits.

It may take a while, but gradually reduce any outstanding balances by overpaying – particularly any card that is accruing interest. Then, once in a while, maybe every other month, apply for a new credit card. If it is a 0% balance transfer card, then transfer and clear existing balances where you are paying interest charges. Your aim should be to reduce your total borrowing and eradicate any borrowing where you pay interest, except for example mortgages because in fact your tenant pays for that anyway.

Summary – good habits for managing your credit cards effectively

- Obtain your credit reports and credit scores regularly – at least every other month and check the information.
- Minimise the number of applications you make to a maximum of one a month and fewer than three in six months (even that could be high).
- Do not reapply if you have just been turned down – wait until you get your credit reports, repair the problem and then wait again before continuing.
- *Always* set up a direct debit payment and then overpay each month as you see fit.
- Keep a spreadsheet and track each card: know your credit limit, know when you last asked for an increase, know when your 0% deal runs out and clear that card first.
- Aim to bring your gearing ratio down by making focused payments.
- Clear any cards that are accruing interest charges as a priority.
- Remember, good debt is for purchases that earn you money, for example a property purchase or refurbishment, and bad debt is the purchase of goods or services that reduce in value and cost you money.
- Finally, whatever you are going to invest in when using your credit card, you must know how you will get the money back to repay your cards.

How it works in practice

When I was in my poor phase as a single mother, literally counting every single 10 pence piece I spent, the credit card was my saviour. I put my money in a high-rate deposit account, spent everything I could on my credit card. Wait, let me rephrase that. I made every payment I could by credit card –

while still knowing my budget and my income. I then cleared the credit card every month in full from the savings account – one withdrawal.

At the end of the year, the bank gave me between £60 and £100 interest for managing my money – which the girls and I spent on our summer holidays and having fun. It might not seem like a lot, but it was a great return for relatively little effort, in a time when my budget for food and entertainment was very limited!

In early 2000, I started to play the 0% off-set game. To do this, you needed an 'Off-set' or 'One' mortgage account (at the time of writing Woolwich, Virgin and Halifax offer them). Essentially, all your money is totalled up every month and the total debt (your mortgage) and your total savings (wages, account balance, etc.) counteract one another.

For example, if you had a £100,000 mortgage and £5,000 joint income, then at the start of each month you only owe £95,000. The next day, after a few bills were paid, you might have had only £4,500 in your account, so now you owed £95,500 and that was the figure you paid your mortgage interest on. However, you didn't earn interest on your savings. It's brilliant in today's market where you are better off off-setting your mortgage, as mortgage interest is 3–6% and savings interest only 1–2%.

The pitfalls

Using credit cards is potentially a risky strategy if you do not know how to use them properly. However, throughout this chapter I have explained and shown examples of how you can monitor and improve your credit rating, borrow money from credit cards often at 0% and extend the use of your own personal cash reserves, plus a whole range of techniques to protect you and your credit rating. Now, before you actually start using credit cards to invest in property, you need to clearly understand your actual investment strategy and how you are going to pay back this loan.

The money borrowed from a credit card, if done well, is a loan at 0% for a limited period of time. You must have in place one, if not two, strategies to clear that debt in full before the end of the term, otherwise you will be paying close to 29% in interest. This strategy must only be used where you know that you can remortgage a renovated property or that you can sell or remortgage a buy-to-let property and release funds to clear the debt.

Credit cards are a brilliant way to extend money and, if they are used correctly, they can increase your credit profile, which enables more lending. If used properly, they are a superb resource of quick and often very cheap funds that can enhance your personal cashflow, making deals more manageable and ultimately more profitable. Remember, always plan what you intend to spend the money on and know how you are going to release the funds back out to repay the borrowing.

Understanding how credit cards work and their impact on your credit score is an easy way to learn about debt and its consequences in preparation for larger mortgage loan commitments. This will be invaluable in ensuring you are prepared to face the mortgage lenders secruity.

This whole chapter has been about money, debt and leverage. Understanding how money works, what lenders want and how your credit score is calculated is like finance 101 and should really be taught in school. Share this information with family members. It is so easy to damage a credit score and then your whole investing career will grind to a halt.

Chapter 5 What lenders want

Now you have mastered the concept of good and bad debt, and created your own money management system, through your personal financial equilibrium and credit card lists, you can start to expand your understanding of what lenders want.

In the end, with new legislation prohibiting joint ventures (Chapter 6) and the expense of bridging finance (Chapter 7), the easiest option for most deals is to access cash for investment through a mortgage or remortgage. That means you have to understand what lenders want.

There are hundreds of banks and mortgage lenders in the market place and they all have slightly different asset and borrowing criteria.

If you ask Google how many banks there are in the world, the answer is over a million. On the one hand, this is encouraging because if one turns you down, then you can simply approach another. It can also seem overwhelming: the challenge of how to approach banks, which ones to pick and what to say.

There is another question: should you use a commercial bank as your lender instead of the off-the-shelf buy-to-let lenders? The best reason to use commercial funding is because they will consider you as a complete person or business, unlike mortgage lenders who see you as a credit score and a specific property. They also 'create' or offer you a lending product that is bespoke to the risk that you present. This means that the more successful they consider you and the lower risk you present, then the more preferential the terms of the loan. I cover this a little later on the next page.

When approaching these business-orientated banks, you will need to present yourself differently – you will need to prepare. The banks are going to want to get to know you on an individual basis and to meet you face to face. They will want details of your existing business and investments, details of your income, expenditure, assets and liabilities (hence the inclusion of Chapter 3). They are, of course, going to consider your credit history, which may show lots of credit cards or mortgage applications may even a lower score. This will not go against you to the degree it does when applying to an ordinary 'production-line' mortgage lender.

If this sounds daunting, one approach is to speak to your broker and explain that you want to approach a commercial bank. They will be able to help and advise you. If not, do it yourself. You have nothing to lose and everything to gain.

Commercial lending or a mortgage – What's the difference? What's the point?

In some ways there is no difference and I will explain why in a minute. Where there is a difference, it is in the philosophy or culture of the organisations that are lending you the money, and that's very noticeable. The banks are old and, in some senses, old-fashioned institutions. They are a contradiction of highly cautious and, yet, extraordinary risk taking.

When you start a conversation with a bank about commercial lending, they will want to follow a very similar process to a mortgage lender. First, the banks will want to know that you are a safe business for the money they are going to lend you. So they will check your credit score, but, more importantly, they will want to meet you face to face (initially) to understand your business model – how it works, where you make money and why it is a good idea.

As you can imagine, this is much more in depth and initially time consuming than applying for a decision in principle (DIP), but may be well worth being considered as a whole entity.

Second, the banks will want to know that they can obtain security for the money they are going to lend you. They will take, in principle, anything of a similar value. This means it does not have to be the actual house you are buying. It could be another unencumbered property, shares, cash savings or, if you are in that market, even gold deposits can be used as collateral. In its simplest form, they will carry out a survey on the investment property.

Now the bank will discuss terms for the lending. These are negotiable! Which means, within reason, the better business proposition you are and the less risk you present, the more preferential the agreed rates.

There are several components to a commercial loan:

1. **The exposure or loan to value** – In simple terms, how much the bank is prepared to lend you against the collateral you are offering. At the moment, they are mostly offering a maximum of 70%. However, you might be able to find higher.

2. **The cost of the money or the interest rate** – Now it is important to be careful here, because most commercial lending is on a capital and repayment basis, not interest-only as with buy-to-let mortgages. Banks use phrases like 'pay rate', which means they will offer you a pay rate of 3.5%, for example, over the base rate (which is currently 0.5%), giving a total loan rate of 4% capital and repayment. (This will feel like a rate of 7%+ if it was an interest-only equivalent loan.)

3. **Coverage** – This means that you must have sufficient income (rent) to cover the cost of repaying the debt. Banks express this as a percentage. In a normal mortgage, they look for 125% coverage. All banks will be different but, essentially, they do not count the full annual rent as income, they assume a percentage of void and maintenance costs. So they may only consider 70% of rental income and then expect that to cover the loan cost by a rate of 140%, for example. You will need to really understand this part of your agreement, otherwise you may find that none of your deals will actually be acceptable.

4. **Finally, there is the term of the loan** – Just as with normal mortgages, this will be based on age. However, because the bank assumes that you will keep the loan and clear it in full through monthly payments (capital and repayment), then this can make your monthly payments quite high and, in turn, affect your ability to provide rental cover. They will refer to the 'amortization' of the loan – how the capital portion of your mortgage payment reduces the actual debt.

This does sound complicated but is in fact really easy to understand, when once again you put yourself in the position of the lender. They want to lend money safely, knowing that you can afford to repay the debt, and, if not, that they have sufficient security to recoup their money if need be.

Why is commercial lending a good idea?

1. Much cheaper fees. Unlike mortgage companies, banks do not charge 2–3.5% admin fees – fees can be just a few hundred pounds. However, the surveys can cost about £500 instead of £300.

2. Banks do not operate a 'six-month rule' on commercial lending. So they do not care if the previous owner only bought the property three months ago.

3. Banks do not charge 'early redemption charges' (ERC). Therefore, although there is a term (length) to the loan, you are not tied into that lending product like you are with a buy-to-let mortgage.

Now look at points 2 and 3 above together. You can buy any property you like (providing it meets the lending criteria), and then either resell it on the open market or remortgage it after refurbishment at closer to its full market value.

This will be very useful if you elect to use certain investment techniques discussed later in the book.

How did I use commercial funding?

In early 2009, I started to approach high street banks. Initially, I took the attitude (to help build my confidence) that I was interviewing them to see which bank could offer me the best service and help my business grow. From the outset, I was well prepared with a presentation and a business plan.

As I progressed to my third 'interview', I learnt through listening to their questions what interested the bank most, and then focused on supplying only that information and the answers to their questions.

Initially I opened an account with an experienced branch manager, but soon realised that I needed a more immediate service. Branch managers often look after upwards of 250 businesses. I eventually met and transferred my business to a relationship manager in central London. The service operation was completely different. He worked with a maximum of 50 businesses and had his own dedicated administrator. He also worked with businesses that turned over in excess of £1million per annum. It was a totally different type of relationship all together.

Once I had established this relationship I could use commercial funding to buy a property for effectively no money down with their full knowledge and understanding. How? I would ask the bank for a remortgage on a property that I currently did not own but that I actually intended to buy. Let me break that down. I would find a suitable property, make my offer to the seller and get it accepted in the normal way. I would then apply for a remortgage rather than a mortgage from the bank.

The bank would carry out a credit check, instruct the survey and eventually make the official offer in the normal way. However, the surveyor would be examining the property with the remortgage value in mind. I never told him the purchase price because I was not buying, I was remortgaging.

Once I had the offer for the remortgage in my hands, I would go ahead and buy the property for cash at the under market value. Within a week, my solicitor would then carry out the remortgage.

Two minor points: we waited a week so that the solicitor could process all the sale papers and then properly remortgage the property; I used my off-set mortgage mentioned at the end of Chapter 4 on page 35 to temporarily fund the purchase.

This was all legal and with the bank's knowledge. They knew I would have only owned the property for under a month – they did not have a six-month rule so this did not matter. I used the bank's survey and the bank's remortgage offer as my personal security checks before I bought. I never bought without having an offer in place to enable me to pull my money back out and repay my off-set mortgage.

I was able to buy and remortgage properties i.e. without a kitchen (I just installed one in between purchase and remortgage) and I was able to buy tired probate properties to redecorate.

After six to nine months, I rechecked the lending rates in the market and the current values of the property and remortgaged for a second time. This time the property was remortgaged to a normal buy-to-let lender because the loan was then on an interest-only basis. This resulted in a dramatically improved cashflow.

The door closed on this approach of remortgaging at full market value in 2011. However, commercial lending is still a great way to buy a property without paying early redemption charges or being liable to the six-month rule. This lending is perfect for refurbishing and flipping small properties quickly without incurring penalties. Or if you are planning to constantly flip properties you could consider bridging finance discussed in Chapter 7.

I continually seek out commercial banks that are open-minded to building relationships with property investors and business owners. I would recommend that investors based inside the M25 – buying local properties – check out MetroBank. They are a new London-based bank that is set on doing business differently – at the very least they offer business accounts that are charge free!

What lenders want – any credit card company, buy-to-let lender or commercial bank – is to know the following:

- Are you the owner of a sound business, well justified with appropriate experience?
- Are you an experienced investor, home owner or business owner?
- Can you provide appropriate levels of collateral, either through the investment property or other ways?
- How much of your own cash are you willing to invest – to risk?
- Can you afford to pay back the loan, through the rent on the property?
- What other income sources do you have – a job or a business?
- What does the internet say about your business, the bank may check your website?

Ultimately, the lender wants to know whether you are going to be a good customer from whom they can make money.

Certainly in my case, banks really liked the fact that Bob was employed and had a regular income – this provided additional security and peace of mind.

They obviously wanted us to transfer our business account to them. They were happy that we deposited a cash lump sum in the account (which we later drew out over a couple of months and paid back to our off-set mortgage).

Think like a professional investor, present yourself as a serious and knowledgeable business owner, show the bank that you know what you are talking about and have a track record of success, or that you are planning to have a track record of success.

Chapter 6 Understanding joint venture legislation

In January 2014 the legislation governing unregulated investment opportunities came into effect. While Policy Statement PS13/3 applies to the wider market and a whole range of unregulated investments, it was triggered, at least in part, by yet another property investment club offering massive returns but not following through. Billions of pounds are rumoured to have been lost in just one individual investment opportunity.

While this book is about how to use other people's money to invest in property, the strategies and applications, it is also very much about the pros, cons and implications of financial investment strategies.

If you are planning to use any funds for property investment purposes that are not your own personal savings then you need to consider all the consequences and risks very carefully. I know I would be totally devastated if anything negative had happened to the funds I have invested over the years. Not just because of any potential lost money, but also because of the failure to fulfil on an investment promise to family or friends.

The mistakes or gambles of certain individuals and companies has meant that the Financial Conduct Authority (FCA) has now added the responsibility, or recommendation and investment of funds, to the role of the financial advisors that help release the funds for investment.

So whether you are remortgaging or using pension funds, the financial advisors helping you access those funds will need to be sure of the investment opportunity you are planning to invest in, and be sure of your ability to absorb the risk if anything should go wrong.

There are certain key characteristics that an investor must adhere to, they are wrapped up in a phrase 'high net worth or sophisticated investor'.

The regulations mean that you cannot discuss or induce investment with a non-family member unless and until:

a. You are registered with the FCA and have the required qualifications to give financial advice.

b. Failing that, you establish beyond doubt that the person/s you are talking to:

1. Has an annual salary of £100,000+.

2. Has independent assets of £250,000+ (not including equity in their main residence).

3. Is employed in an investment capacity in a financial service industry i.e. a professional investor.

4. Is a bone fide provable angel investor in business start-ups.

5. Is a family member.

6. Is a friend of long standing i.e. several years.

If you have been active in using private money, a visit to this link[6] to find out what changes the FCA have made is advisable.

If we just focus on property investment and the direct impact of the legislation then this prohibits offering property JVs, or joint ventures, unless your potential JV partner meets the criteria above. It also means that any existing JVs should be brought to a close.

While this might be nearly impossible to regulate on a day-to-day basis, if a deal does go wrong, investors now have a point of contact and legislation to help them pursue purveyors of high risk investments or deals that fail to deliver on their promises.

Even inviting a 'stranger' to lend you money or host a mortgage is a high risk – there is a risk they could lose their investment and while we all like to believe that we have an iron clad deal, things do go wrong.

---

6   http://www.fca.org.uk/static/documents/policy-statements/ps13-03.pdf

Case study 1

Why JVs are a bad idea for the investor

Facebook is always a source of deals gone wrong and this particular case involved a property sourcer in the north I had met 4–5 years ago (but did not train). An investor was offered the deal where they became the mortgagee on the property and the property sourcer was to manage the refurbishment and letting.

Following the purchase of the property in the investor's name, the property sourcer received funds of £20,000 in two payments, paid directly to them, to carry out the refurbishment and the letting. The deal structure meant that the property sourcer would then benefit from 50% of the capital uplift in property value upon remortgage and retain half the rental income for the management.

Needless to say something went wrong, months and thousands of pounds later the property was still empty, the work paid for remained unfinished. With the mortgage payments and costs piling up the investor travelled to the property, tried to contact the sourcer and of course discovered the full extent of their mistake. The property sourcer was on holiday, the property still unfinished although more than £40,000 had been paid for the refurbishment over the last five months. The investor had already remortgaged their home and had the mortgage on the investment property to pay. It was costing them more than they could afford without the promised rental income!

Case study 2

Why JVs don't make sense as a business

I always remember a call I received a couple of years ago from a property sourcer that had just completed on a deal and after reading the first edition of this book realised that maybe the deal was not such a good idea. They wondered if I could help.

Essentially they had approached a potential client with money to invest to buy a property. They used the investor's cash to buy the property and renovate it. The property sourcers would then benefit from half the rental profit in return for the finding, fixing and filling process and the ongoing management.

In brief the property sourcers would earn £125pcm, that's £1,500 after the first twelve months (and that includes the initial four months to find and fix the property). The investor was using all his own cash to buy and renovate the property. After a deduction from the rent of £208 to cover the equivalent of the mortgage, the investor also received half the rent per month.

In fact the investor was getting a total of £333 per month (£208 plus half the remaining £250 profit) £3,996 on his total cash investment of £50,000 (plus four months of no income during renovation and the cost of the refurbishment as well) that's just 8%.

If the investor had used a mortgage it would have cost £156.25 at 5% per month leaving £301.75 net profit. They would have had £12,500 left in the house as cash deposit (plus the same refurbishment costs) giving 29% ROI on the £12,500 cash used.

On top of this, the property sourcer or JV partner (as in fact that's what they were) would have earned approximately £3–5,000 within five months as a sourcing fee and not had to manage the property either.

Consequences: time and money

These are just two case studies to show you how much better it is for both parties to have a clear arrangement where the property sourcer's job is to find a good deal (that fits a prescribed model) and then offer a specific level of management through the buying process for a fee. The investor then owns the property and all the rental profit. Both parties earn more, more quickly and without a long-term legal or contractual entanglement.

This is the type of service I offer my clients and I discuss this very different approach in Chapter 17. The critical difference being that I charge a flat fee for my time, paid on completion, meanwhile my clients keep hold of their money and pay all members of my professional team directly for work delivered.

The fee is for my time, I effectively treat this service as a job and I earn the equivalent of an hourly rate. On average a property from offer to fully let takes about ten days of work. Of course it takes more time to actually find the right property for sale in the first place. Unlike a full-time job, when I work I get paid and when I don't – I don't get paid so that means I can manage the impact on my lifestyle both in terms of time and income – I have a choice.

Sourcing or joint ventures, if you do offer any, will definitely come with a commitment to deliver on a promise, like any of the techniques and strategies in this book. There is a moral, and should be a contractual, obligation to deliver on the service and returns promised.

Now with legislation, these sorts of joint venture deals are governed by the FCA who can investigate and support those that are at risk. To offer any form of unregulated investment or property joint venture you must be able to demonstrate that your joint venture partner has high net worth and is 'sophisticated' according to the criteria at the start of this chapter.

Simply put when you find a good deal that you can't fund directly yourself or with the help of family – source the deal to someone else for a fee. It's easier, quicker and a better rate of return for you both. Anyone thinking of investing should have a detailed conversation with a professional financial advisor before making a commitment.

Chapter 7 Bridging loans – recycle your cash

What is bridging finance and why do people use it?

Bridging finance or a bridging loan is basically money borrowed for a specific, short-term business reason. A bridging loan is a formal agreement where either an individual or a company lends you money for a fee, for a period of time, which is secured against a property. This formal approach to borrowing other people's money is not a strategy I have personally used, though I have worked with mentees as they have progressed through deals. I have also bridged my own deals through my own cash.

So, in some ways, a 'bridge' or bridging loan is a mini mortgage used to bridge and span a short period of time before more permanent loans are put in place, such as a buy-to-let mortgage or a resale is concluded (flipping). Having used the words 'short period', I should explain this can be anywhere from one month to nine months (or longer – but then you really need to have a great reason to do this).

Bridging loan companies are not bound by the Council of Mortgage Lenders' rules. Most bridging companies are just like mortgage lenders in so much as their lending is just based on a percentage of the purchase price. However, there are more enlightened bridgers that will consider lending based on a percentage of the value of the property.

Typically, a bridging company would be prepared to lend 70% of the purchase price; the more enlightened ones lend 65% of the open market value. A few will lend 70% of the valuation or 85% of the purchase price whichever is lower. There are other permutations that a specific bridger may lend, but the conclusion is that you almost always have to be putting in at least some cash as bridgers won't want to take all of the risk. You may have agreed a purchase price of £65,000 on a property worth (according to valuation) £100,000, for example. Therefore, in this case, the enlightened bridging company would lend £65,000 as if they were lending against value not the purchase price.

If that sounds confusing, well it can be. If you are not familiar with using bridging, it can be a lot safer if you use an experienced bridging finance broker who will know which lender will lend what on which types of property.

When bridging makes sense

Bridging finance is often used when a property is unmortgageable for some reason. Perhaps the property does not have a bathroom or a kitchen, so it is classed as uninhabitable. Another reason might be because the property transaction needs to complete quickly, such as when buying at an auction.

In the example of a property that is uninhabitable, the investor will have applied for a regular buy-to-let mortgage, but it has been granted with the condition of a full retention until certain works are completed. The investor would then use bridging finance to buy the property, fit the kitchen or complete refurbishment works, and then ask the lender to reinspect and release funds to clear the bridge.

Investors that understand how to use bridging finance can often pick up a tasty deal from an estate agent when the buyer has pulled out because it had a bad survey. If the agent knows you can come to the rescue when a deal has 'fallen out of bed', you can save the day and keep both seller and agent happy.

I mentioned the Council of Mortgage Lenders (CML) above; they are cause for another use of bridging. A few years ago it was easy to buy a property, carry out a refurbishment and then remortgage when the works were complete – maybe within two months or so. Then the CML decided that properties could not be mortgaged or remortgaged in under six months. This means that the whole process of buying and refurbishing (discussed in Chapter 10) has been slowed down through this rule.

Now if the numbers make sense you could buy with a bridging loan – refurbish a property and then 'remortgage' using a certain (limited) pool of lenders that do not demand the condition that six months' ownership is met. I will show you the practical applications a bit later.

As with every method described in this book, the critical point is to know how you are going to repay the bridging loan. There are huge penalties for overrunning on the agreed timescales. Let's look at some of the costs involved.

So what is it going to cost – one arm or two legs?

Bridging loans are notoriously expensive. Interest is sometimes calculated on a daily but mostly on a monthly interest rate. So, for example, you may be offered 1.0–1.5% per month, but this is actually approaching 12–18% per annum. Quite a shock when a buy-to-let mortgage would cost approximately 5% per annum.

How do the numbers actually work?

Most bridging companies will charge for the following:

- Arrangement fee – this is typically 2% of the loan, a one-off upfront payment.
- Legal and admin costs – usually £500–£1,000, which covers the bridging company's legal fees – you will still need to budget for your own costs.
- Ongoing interest – this can range from 1–1.5% a month. Of course, how you pay the interest is entirely down to the company. One or two bridgers will say it can be paid monthly, but most experienced investors will look to get an agreement to have the 'interest rolled up'. This means the lender will add the monthly payments to the loan but deduct them at the point the loan commences. This does mean that you don't have to actually make payments each month during the loan.
- Exit costs – there is often an exit fee that is up to one month's interest of the loan. However, there are some bridging companies that do not charge this fee – it is worth checking.

How interest is charged

As mentioned previously, most bridging companies charge interest on a monthly basis, which means if you use your bridge for two months and one day, you will be charged three months' interest. However, there are some flexible bridging companies that charge interest on a daily basis. It's worth looking out for these firms, as they tend to work out cheaper in the long term, especially if you are renovating and you are ahead of schedule.

Having said that, if you are in a position to settle ahead of schedule and if all the payments had been taken when the loan commenced, most bridgers give you a rebate for settling early.

So do the figures work for you?

As you can see, bridging loans can work out very expensive. Sometimes it's worth it and sometimes it's not. As an investor, you need to know that you can afford the monthly fees associated with having a bridging loan, which could quite easily be around £2,000 a month on a typical £100,000 loan.

You will also need to be very aware that any overrun in the project refurbishment or delay in a sale will impact significantly on your profit, and may even wipe it out completely! If you exceed the term of your bridging loan, the interest can double. Your success in this finance strategy will depend on understanding the maths of the deal. Check with a bridging expert and, of course, check the resources section at www.TheSourcersApprentice.com for our Deal Analyser Workshop DVD.

What is your exit strategy?

How are you going to repay the money to the bridging company?

The first question any bridging company will always ask is: 'What is your exit strategy?' This means they want to know how you are going to pay their money back. Why do they ask this? Because they only want you to have their money for a short amount of time. They are focused on lending money, not investing in property long term.

So if you have been preapproved for a buy-to-let mortgage, which will in effect buy out their debt, you can demonstrate a level of credit worthiness and an exit strategy through the one offer letter.

In many cases, the bridging company will also want to see that you have a track record as an experienced investor and so this particular strategy is not always available as your first approach to using other people's money to invest in property. Some bridging companies will want you, as an individual wanting to borrow money, to have experience in investing with three to five investment properties already in your portfolio as reassurance, but not always.

As an investor, you would need to show what you want to use the money for and how long you need it. Remember the bridging company wants to know how its money is being used and when they can plan to lend it out again. It usually takes 5–10 days to receive the funds once your request for a bridging loan has been approved. That's the thing about bridging, it is very quick.

You should speak to your financial advisor to check that you are making a sound financial decision before you go ahead and invest using bridging finance. The bridging company is there primarily to lend money and make a profit, they are not financial advisors. It is important to choose your advisor carefully. Your normal financial advisor may do a terrific job for you on most of your finances but they may rarely get involved in bridging finance. As mentioned previously in this case you may do better by seeking out a specialist bridging broker.

Your advisor and the bridging company will then carry out the normal due diligence on you, your strategy and the property. Ultimately, the bridging company needs to be sure that you are able to keep up and manage the loan repayments before they lend you the money (if you are paying the interest on a regular monthly basis). The approval process will, of course, include a survey on the property.

As mentioned already, the bridging company will require adequate security for their loan; this will mostly take the form of a charge on the property you wish to buy but can also be a charge on your home, or a number of properties in your investment portfolio. Taking charges over properties other than the one you are buying is usually only done when you are trying to buy a property using little or none of your own hard cash, but have plenty of equity in other properties you already own.

This provides a level of 'comfort' to the lender. Make no mistake, if you do not pay on time, they will ultimately move to repossess the security they hold a legal charge on. If you do overrun and you keep the bridger informed, most will work with you to find a way to pay them back but you must be clear they will repossess if a solution can't be found. So be very careful about the terms of the deal you agree.

Where do they get the money to lend?

It really depends on the bridging company. Some use their funds from a pot of money they hold, and some have funding lines with major financial institutions like High Street banks. There are other companies that use money lent to them.

Bridging companies may use money lent to them by savvy members of the general public. For example, someone could have come into some capital and identified that they have a lump sum of money that they are not going to use for six or seven months or even two to three years. They would talk with the finance company and discuss what opportunities are available to invest in at the moment.

The savvy investor would receive half of the upfront fee, and half of the exit fee, which is a significant proportion of fees and a great return on their investment. This is considerably more than they would get from a bank or building society. Of course, there is the risk that there could be an overrun and they may not receive the payment when it is due, but the bridging company's role is to mitigate against this happening.

Specific and specialist

This strategy is used to support a specific investment approach. For example, I have a contact who buys property at auction, uses his build team to renovate the property and then resells the property to other investors or to the general public.

By using bridging finance and selling deals in this way you could still be a property trader, where the size of your portfolio, or lack of equity in your portfolio, limits your ability to access additional mortgage lending. Bridging does not hinder the sale of the property because you are not tied in to fixed-term mortgage products. There are definite advantages. Although there will be a restricted number of lenders that the new buyer can use because of the six-month rule – this applies to residential as well as investor mortgages.

Disadvantages come in the form of huge financial penalties for overstepping an agreed time frame – so do your calculations precisely and then factor in some extra time because these things always take longer than they are meant to.

Kevin Wright[7], a long-time friend and financial expert shared some of his top tips with me about how to make bridging work.

1. Think like a cash buyer – bridging finance can allow you to move as fast as a cash buyer, so start thinking and acting like one.

2. Look for problems, unmortgageable properties – most buyers drop out when they can't get a mortgage, even some investors; leaving the way clear for cash buyers and savvy investors to pick up some great deals and become the agent's best friend.

---

7   www.recycleyourcash.co.uk   www.positivepropertyfinance.co.uk

3. If you are looking to buy at auction, focus on making pre and post auction offers – when you are not influenced by the auction day bidding frenzy.

4. Look for sellers that need to sell rather than want to sell – the speed at which you can complete using bridging finance will be of greater appeal to this group.

5. Focus on the opportunity, not the cost – look for projects that can yield a significant profit, way more than the cost of financing it.

6. Think bridging finance before you think about trying to get JV finance (Chapter 6) – check out the cost of using a bridging lender, it will rarely eat up the 50% of your profit that a JV investor funding your deal normally wants.

Cost to establish, time implications and impact on lifestyle

Bridging finance as a funding strategy is fairly quick and easy, subject to your credit worthiness and the details of the planned investment. There are no real implications at this point other than you have a time-sensitive debt to service. The impact on your time, your lifestyle and the risks that come with this financial strategy will be influenced by the investment technique you choose to invest the money into.

At this point, if you change your mind – or do not find a suitable deal – then you could repay the bridging loan and just suffer the cost of the administration fees to set up the loan and the cost of the survey.

Chapter 8 Release money from your home

'Equity release' is a term that means to release (through mortgage or remortgage) money (equity) from your own home, or another family member's home. This is possible where the current value of your mortgage is considerably less than the current value of your home. So, for example, if you bought your house a few years ago and have an outstanding £50,000 mortgage and the house is now worth £250,000, then there is up to £200,000 equity in the home that could be released. You will only be able to access 75% of this through mortgage or remortgage because of lender restrictions on loan-to-value ratios.

Exploiting the leverage this strategy offers and using it to purchase other properties is exactly what I discussed in Chapter 3. This, like all of the other strategies, can be combined to make ever more creative deals, but let's keep it simple for now. It does take some thought and some planning, but is by far the easiest way to use other people's money to invest in property.

It pays for itself

In the ultimate of all 'none of your own money in the deal' deals – using other people's money – this strategy actually enables you to borrow the funds against your home. You will know the effective cost of borrowing or using that money in advance, because it will have been released through a mortgage, a draw down facility, or a further advance.

You can also calculate the cashflow from the proposed investment deal and make sure that it can cover that cost of borrowing. This should leave a surplus or profit. In effect, this strategy enables you to fund deposits on great cashflowing deals.

By using other people's money or releasing equity from your own house, you can increase the size of your property portfolio. By gaining control of another asset and collecting the additional cashflow, you leverage money from the bank to put additional funds into your pocket. Eventually, you can repay the original loan using the capital gain as property prices eventually increase in value or save the profit from the rent and repay the loan more quickly.

The other 'selling' point for equity release is the leverage of your own home.

How does this work? Your house will continue to slowly and gradually increase in value. That money or value is meaningless unless you release it through a sale or an equity release.

This, again, is where understanding good and bad debt is essential. I know I have visited hundreds of houses that were bought for £50,000 five to seven years ago. I can see, using online valuation services, that they have been revalued and remortgaged. I can also see when I go in the house that they have had a new kitchen fitted and bought a flat screen TV. I also know that within 12–18 months of the remortgage they were repossessed!

Why? Because that remortgage or equity release was bad debt; the money was spent on items that did not generate income to contribute towards paying off the interest due. I know what you are shouting, 'The kitchen added value to the house!' Well, maybe, but if they did not release the additional value and pay back the debt, as a professional investor would have done. All they have done is treated themselves to a new luxury kitchen. Good debt is where the money borrowed is used to leverage more income over and above the cost of borrowing.

Only good debt

The money you release must be and will be good debt. Surely you would only commit your own home or that of your parents when you knew for certain that the rental income would pay the interest and leave you with a surplus. You also need to know that you can remortgage the new investment properties in 6–12 months and pay back or recycle the funds into more cashflowing deals.

Alternatively, if you have a sufficient equity pot, you may be buying outright and either flipping or remortgaging in six months on to the open buy-to-let mortgage market.

Remember that assets are things that give you a regular cashflow; when looking at a deal you should look for the cashflow and not just for the potential capital gain.

Interest rates, cashflow and release – they are the rules

Always do your research on the interest rates thoroughly for any money you plan to borrow through equity release. The property that you are considering releasing equity from will mostly likely already have a mortgage. If not, then just get the best rate possible. However, if it is mortgaged, then you need to understand the product you are on; your broker can help with this.

Don't be too quick to remortgage as you may lose a very preferential rate and end up costing yourself a lot of money over time. Working with your parents or older family members may be easier, as they will most likely be mortgage free.

Now invest wisely and always look for the cashflow. This is obvious but all the more important when you must use the surplus cashflow to cover the cost of the equity release as well as provide yourself with a profit. And always make sure you have a plan of when and how you will get the money back. If you are involving other family members, make sure they understand. Ensure that you have taken out suitable life insurance and put it in trust to protect the people you have borrowed money from.

It is important to understand where you want to be in five years' time. A good business strategy and a good exit strategy are crucial.

Creating money out of nothing

Let me explain our strategy for using other people's money. We released £200,000 from my parents' unencumbered house. The cost of the mortgage was approximately £500 per month. I then used the £200,000 to fund the deposit and purchase costs of seven investment properties. The deposit and total purchase costs including broker, through solicitor, various fees and the refurbishment budget came to just under £30,000 per property.

This also covered the cost of letting the property – all the certificates, letting agent fees and two months of mortgage costs, which is the maximum time I allowed to refurbish and fill a property .

Each of these properties is let, netting a profit of £250–£300 per month after the cost of the main mortgage, the letting agent fee and insurance. (In total, this is the mortgage plus about a 15% budget.) This surplus, on average £250, then contributes towards the initial cost of borrowing the £200,000 investment pot. The total overall profit across all seven properties is £1,750 less the cost of the £500 mortgage per month. Let me just say that one more time – I make £1,250 profit from mortgaging my parents' house. And this is only one example.

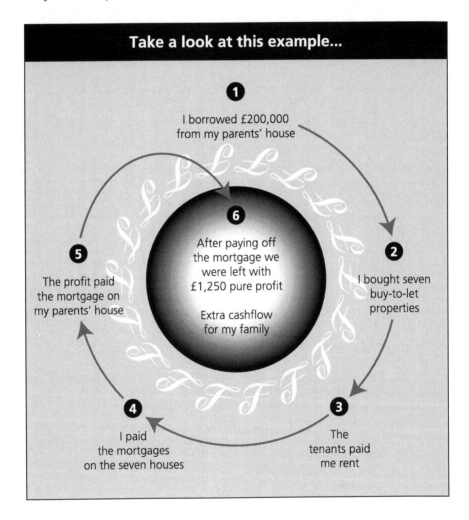

Take a look at this example...

1 I borrowed £200,000 from my parents' house

2 I bought seven buy-to-let properties

3 The tenants paid me rent

4 I paid the mortgages on the seven houses

5 The profit paid the mortgage on my parents' house

6 After paying off the mortgage we were left with £1,250 pure profit

Extra cashflow for my family

Case study 1

Funding a peaceful retirement

A client with grown-up children and a current unencumbered house wants to move to her dream house in the next year. So, rather than sell her current home I costed out that she could release £150,000 that would be covered by rental income. With the £100,000 she could invest in a couple of properties that would generate £1,000–£1,500 of rental profit. This profit would pay for the remortgage on the primary house and the mortgage on the new smaller home (using the remaining £50,000 as a deposit).

I helped the client create a property portfolio for herself (rental income) and her children and grandchildren (through the assets) of one main residential property, the primary house rented out and a further two buy-to-let investment properties. In the long term, they can be moved into a family trust for the grandchildren. Best of all she lives rent free – forever!

Case study 2

Taking care of family

In the second example my client needed to care for elderly relatives. So money was released from the family home and invested in buy-to-let property. The income (profit) generated from investment covered the cost of the mortgage on the family home and the care home fees.

In addition, the home is still retained so should circumstances change they have the flexibility to move back in or sell in years to come.

Paying it back

Staying with the example of my parents' house for a moment, each property is on a one or two-year mortgage product. As each property becomes eligible for remortgage, I will check the valuations and, if sensible (because property values have increased), I will remortgage and then either repay the mortgage on my parents' house or more likely reinvest the money into yet more properties.

How does the equity release owner benefit?

Now if you consider my strategy described above, you could offer your family member a share of that profit. If you share, for example a 70/30 split, you personally could still net £875 a month and your family or friend take £375 a month.

In my case, I paid a 'fee' each time I used the money, as splitting the profit, didn't seem such a great offer. The 'lending fee' was a tax-deductible expense to the business. As long as I keep the annual total paid to my parents under their tax-free allowance, then they don't pay tax either – a win-win situation for all involved.

So what's the risk? A word of caution

We have been taught by parents and peers to pay our mortgages off and that debt is bad, but, as you know, it is important to make the distinction.

Some people, quite rightly, have concerns about releasing equity from a property, especially if it is your own home or your parents' home. You need to carefully consider the risk and consequences affecting the investment you will make.

Of course you will need to stress test both mortgages to ensure you completely understand the impact of inevitable interest rate rises.

It can also involve some legal paperwork to sign deeds over from one person to another, so that there is an income-earning person on the mortgage. It can make partners who are not educated in the ways of professional property investing feel really uncomfortable and afraid about the future security of their home.

This can all be easily resolved by seeing a financial advisor or a solicitor who will be able to explain that the release is to invest in assets that are income generating. Also, a written description of the investment and repayment process can help you to clarify and explain the property proposal and demonstrate your experience and examples.

You are actually putting yourself in a position where your buy-to-let deal is 100% funded. This means you really must ensure that you have excellent cashflow to cover the cost of the two loans. You will have the primary buy-to-let mortgage and the initial equity release loan (that becomes the deposit).

Personally, I would still want to be receiving at least £200 per month per property after the primary (buy-to-let) mortgage, the equity release mortgage and insurances, etc. have all been paid. Use ROI as a measure and aim to get 10–14% coverage as a minimum.

You may be wondering why am I setting the figure so high. This is because interest rates have never been better; the Bank of England is at 0.5% and can only go up. So if you can't get good cashflow now, then maybe the deal isn't good enough. After all, the whole point of this is to get cash flowing into your pocket!

Cost to establish, time implications and impact on lifestyle

The equity release is fairly quick and easy, subject to your credit worthiness. There are no real implications at this point other than you have a debt to service. The impact on time, lifestyle and additional risk come with the technique you choose to invest the money.

Now if you change your mind or don't decide to invest you could face significant loan repayments on the remortgage of your primary residential property. If the loan is part of a draw down facility then interest is only payable at the point of draw down or use.

You can repay the remortgage, but there might be penalties for early redemption and there will be the cost of the administration of the mortgage and the survey to cover. So now the hard work begins – find cashflowing deals to repay this debt.

Chapter 9 Family money – working together

There are definitely pros and cons associated with borrowing money from family and friends. Some people are reluctant to do so as they feel awkward asking for money, but it is an easy way of getting into the property market. It also provides a great opportunity for the family member or friend to make a better rate of return on the money than they would if it was in the bank. It is really about sharing wealth and opportunities. However given new joint venture legislation PS13/03 discussed in Chapter 6 you need to be very careful how much you borrow and on what terms. Personal loans are still allowed.

Start with an agreement

It is a good idea to draw up a formal agreement right from the start so that everyone involved in the investment loan knows what to expect, when to expect it and it simply makes things less complicated. The level of formality of the agreement is often dictated by the closeness of the family member and not necessarily the amount of money being borrowed. I would at the very least recommend that you just write down what you have agreed.

What should be in the agreement?

Don't make the conditions of borrowing the money over complicated. Start by understanding your deal. Are you planning to buy, refurbish and hold the property as a long-term buy-to-let, with the potential to remortgage and release funds in the next 6–12 months? Or are you planning to buy a property that needs a lot more work, significantly increase its value and then sell (flip) on?

Why does this matter? Well, think about how and when you are going to pay back the money you have borrowed and how much interest, if any, will be paid and when. The strategy you are planning to use will dictate the terms of your offer to your family and friends.

If you are planning to buy, do up and sell, for example, you could reach an agreement where you repay the money on the sale of the property. I would suggest that you also put a fixed and final date at some point in the future for security and clarity's sake.

In many cases where close family members are lending smaller amounts of money there is no conversation about interest payments. Especially if borrowing from parents who will often be more than willing to lend the money.

Where family or friends have a larger amount of money to lend, maybe taking the money from a savings account or releasing it as equity then there needs to be a discussion about how lending money to you will generate more interest for them than a bank or building society. And, of course, you must cover the cost of any borrowing (in the example of equity release).

Again, at this point a simple document stating your names, the amount of the loan, the purpose of the loan, end/repayment date and any interest due is such an easy thing to do.

What if your best-laid plans go wrong?

Be clear in writing what would happen in the unlikely event of a falling out between partners (disagreement). Could the family member demand the money back? Make it clear in writing what the terms and conditions are for every eventuality.

A get-out clause will hopefully never be necessary because part of the process and discussion to create the terms of the loan will show up any potential areas of disagreement. It is vital to your business' success that those people you do business with, add to your success and do not detract from your profit.

I worked with a client recently who was an experienced investor with a medium-sized portfolio. He had bought property with family money and the help of a family member. After changes in the family, including divorce and death, the nature of the relationship changed and the family partner wanted their money back.

The investor came to me for ideas on how to raise the money needed to buy out the family member and get rid of all the stress. The detail of what I suggested is not important – the fact that I helped the investor see that they could increase the cashflow and pay off the family member was a great outcome. The lesson? Even family can fall out!

Now I am going to get morbid

As this money is being borrowed from family and/or friends, in my opinion, you should consider a life insurance policy and maybe even changes to your will. The principle here is not to leave your family in a mess should something unfortunate happen to you. If your daughter had taken out a loan on your behalf or your sister had lent you her savings, would you want them to be out of pocket, even if it was just for a matter of months while the probate was sorted out? It doesn't have to be expensive. Get a simple fixed-term life insurance policy online.

Understanding the deal is the key

Really this is the easiest way to borrow money – you just need to understand your deal, what (how much) you need to get in and how you are planning to get out, your exit strategy. Then present your proposal.

A privately written finance document, can be used to write down and present, professionally, the details of the loan and why the deal would work. Most family members won't even read the document, but it will give you the confidence that you have thought through the deal and that their money is safe. Using a deal analyser can help you get the maths clear in your head and give you the key numbers to present to your potential family banker.

If you look at the maths, you will see just how easy borrowing money from friends and family can be. Imagine that you need £50,000 to pay for the deposit and all the purchasing costs of a property. To ask one person to lend you £50,000 might be a challenge, not only for you, but also for your family member or friend. There are fewer people around with a full £50,000 lying around unused.

Now imagine that a combination of family members (say five to make my maths easy) all lend you £10,000 each. You still have the sum required. Each lender has either spread their risk or lent a smaller amount. Also, if at any point one lender needs their funds back, you only have to replace £10,000 and not a much larger amount. Do you know five friends or family who might be interested in lending you money and earning a higher rate of interest than they would get in a bank?

Our agreement

In my case, I thought through as many variations and eventualities as possible. My family and I created a partnership agreement that clearly laid out how much money each family member would lend the 'pot', what the money could be spent on, how profit would be shared. We discussed what would happen to the investments if one partner died. We made wills and put them into trust, then agreed that the wills would pay the beneficiaries.

Then we agreed what would happen if one partner or investor wanted to leave the agreement before the time agreed. OK, it did take us more than a couple of hours, but that was because there was a lot we all had to consider, contribute and agree. In the end, we not only had a strong partnership but also a reasonable pot of money with which to start investing.

Case study

Family Banking – cashflow capital and equity

The parents of one of my clients lent them £100,000 to invest in a property so that the total pot was £200,000. This was used to buy and refurbish a property.

The final product was split into two properties with the larger part being sold for £300,000. The parents were returned their funds including an additional £50,000 which is an extremely generous interest rate but one that enabled the parents to clear their personal mortgage. The second part of the investment was held to generate cashflow and the client had a total of £225,000 (75% of the £100,000 second property and £150,000, their share of the sold property) to enable them to source their next deal.

So what is the risk? A word of caution

Unlike equity release the funds lent to you will have come from savings. You will definitely help your family by paying more interest than the building societies. However 'stuff' happens and family circumstances change – they may need the money back sooner than planned.

Do not over stretch yourself. Be sure you have a fall-back plan to refund the money if it is needed sooner. Your family is more important than the deal in the end, so the deal must be good for all the family.

Cost to establish, time implications and impact on lifestyle

Borrowing from family members can either be instantaneous or follow a slow process of building trust and changing beliefs. Remember not everyone thinks like you do. Even if they are family they may still hold different beliefs about money.

Again there are no real implications at this point other than you have a debt to service, there won't be monthly payments (or though for a larger sum there may be). The impact on your time, lifestyle and additional risk again come with the technique you choose to invest the money.

At this point, if you need to change your plans, you can repay the loans with no cost implications. Now you need to make that money work for all of you.

Section 3
Investment Techniques

Chapter 10 Refurbish, add value and remortgage

Now I am going to apply the financial strategies already discussed to specific techniques designed to leverage money through property investment. You will be able to see how they work in practice and the cost, time implication and impact on lifestyle.

Essentially the refurbishment and add value technique is the normal buy and hold model. While I do not advocate excessive remortgaging of properties as it can dramatically increase the risk levels in your portfolio, some properties are suitable for refurbishment and remortgage.

The Vanilla buy-to-let

Before I explain how the technique works best let's look at the ordinary buy-to-let property. An example would be any property bought to rent out on a single assured shorthold tenancy contract (AST); a single family let is an example. The property could typically require only a light redecoration and a budget of approximately £5,000 including carpets.

At this point in time (early summer 2014) I find it difficult to imagine where in the country a surveyor would revalue the property at any more than £10,000 over the purchase price during the next six months (if that). This is because outside the M25, purchase prices are still fairly stable and rising only slowly if at all. So why would a coat of paint make the property worth any more that the purchase price plus £10,000? This would make remortgaging unviable.

The Rum and Raison buy-to-let

This type of property would often be advertised as 'in need of modernisation' – a classic estate agent phrase meaning the property has not been updated since the 1980s or earlier.

You would be expecting to buy this property below the average street value. For example if a fully renovated property in the same street sold for £100,000 in the last 1–2 months and this property needed approximately £25,000 of work then I imagine an estate agent would try and sell the property for a cheeky £85,000 expecting a small knock back. Remember that properties are now starting to attract a lot of attention from returning seasoned investors and the Homes under the Hammer viewer, alike. Do not become a 'desperate buyer', falling foul of the estate agent's 'full and final' offer tactics. Hold your nerve when negotiating.

Of course if you do your own marketing, rather than through an estate agent and you can attract a seller directly then you will be able to negotiate a lower price.

Remember if your intention is to buy and refurbish and hold for cashflow and you expect to make a great rental profit when you rent the place out – don't be greedy. Reducing the asking price by £4,000 will only save you £1,000 in cash and might lose you the deal as £4,000 is a great deal of money to most sellers. Use a spreadsheet to understand the impact of small changes in offer price or small errors in refurbishment costs!

If works take three months and the media is right about property optimism then you might expect a revaluation at £100–110,000. Remember the surveyors know the area and can see sold prices and know how much the work you carried out cost! So think carefully about how much you can expect to release on a 75% remortgage, and factor in the costs of solicitor fees and another survey.

So buy, refurbish, add value and remortgage only works (and is financially worth it) on properties where you are carrying out significant works. Adding a new bathroom, a new kitchen, a boiler, maybe windows, or electrics, even adding bathrooms will impact on the genuine value of a property.

Other light touch redecorating deals are not worth remortgaging immediately and will not justify bridging as discussed earlier in Chapter 7.

Making this technique work

The crucial pivot point in making this technique work successfully for you is the numbers! You need to be sure that above all there is still a net cashflow even when the remortgage is stressed to 8% (or higher). There is little point owning a property with none of your own (or family) capital invested in the deal if next year or the year after, when interest rates rise, you have to start paying the mortgage!

Making this technique work depends on four factors. I will outline these in brief and then explain in more detail:

1. Picking the right area – if you are planning to increase a property's value you need to be in an area where the 'ceiling' price of the road does not limit your potential revaluation.

2. Having the right team, from estate agent contacts to builders who can work to the right level of specification (spec).

3. Knowing the numbers. Like in the previous chapters, understanding the numbers of this deal is crucial. This technique involves not only the purchase price, but also the cost of the refurbishment and a small error in judgement here can be very costly. And, of course, understanding the future rental profit.

4. Getting the money back out – what are your two exit strategies?

Picking the right area

This technique, along with the buy-to-sell – flipping (Chapter 11) technique, needs the property to be in a desirable area with potential market growth. There are hundreds, if not thousands, of derelict and boarded properties in the north of England and, yes, they will be cheap. Unfortunately, no amount of money spent on them will enable you to get your investment back because the area, and the market in that area, will not enable you to raise the value sufficiently that you will get your money back out (or enable you to sell quickly for a good price if you have to).

You will find areas where this works, but you need to do your research and know the market. You will need to buy at a significantly low price in order to meet this equation.

Final valuation x 75% = remortgage. The remortgage minus the cost of refurbishment and purchase costs, must equal or be more than the price you pay for the property.

So for example if your refurbished property (and the street value) is worth £100,000 you will only be able to borrow £75,000 on the remortgage (yes there are some loans for 85% loan to value but then you are decreasing the cashflow further and increasing the risk in the portfolio).

If the cost of works were going to be £25,000 (say a new kitchen, bathroom, boiler, electrics, full replaster, redecorate and new carpets) plus the buying costs of the solicitor, broker, surveyor and four months mortgage payments on two properties (using equity release), then you would have to buy the property at £50,000.

Now in six years of property hunting I have only found half a dozen properties where I actually could buy a property for £50,000 in a street where the final valuation was £100,000.

Why? Because most estate agents have favoured investors, who get deals before they hit the market (I am now in that position but it takes hard work and time to develop that level of trust). A lot of investors and builders would buy a property like this for cash – so you would need to operate the bridging technique to help you move quickly enough.

Then you have to get a surveyor who knows you paid £50,000 to give you a revaluation at £100,000 (I would not risk my financial future on a surveyor).

What we aim to achieve in our model is to buy a property at £85–95,000 (in a street worth £100,000) obviously less if we can, but our aim is to own the property not lose it to another investor. Then carry out a genuine £20,000 worth of works, add about £5,000 of costs to buy and hold until it's ready to let. We then want a revaluation of £125–130,000 as a minimum. This way our clients can realise the new value – they only have their original deposit amount still in the deal and we can recoup the cost of the refurbishment. The client still has 10–14% net rental profit each month.

It is vital to our technique that we still have equity in our properties (so that we can enable a quick sale in the future if we need to) and still have a solid cashflowing property that is able to withstand interest rate rises. When we remortgage, we only release some of the cash invested, we don't release it all. The money left in earns an incredible rate of return. Most of my clients are cash rich and not looking for hundreds of houses. They want peace of mind and more cash. Most clients only need 4–10 properties to enable a couple to retire in comfort (subject of course to their hobbies).

To determine the ceiling price of a street, speak to an estate agent about a property before you buy it, you can pretend that you are thinking of selling. (Obviously you need to speak to a different agent from the one who is selling to you!) Ask them what the 'ceiling price' for the street is. What is the highest sale price currently being achieved and what has it reached in the past (before the crash)? This should help you to recognise the maximum price that you will be likely to achieve on sale or remortgage.

It is tough to achieve ceiling price and even harder to break though. Budget and go for the easily achievable prices, even slightly under market value.

Having the right team

A good way to find properties that are for sale, at less than market value, is to develop a relationship with estate agents. Some property trainers give the impression that you can just go to an estate agency, walk in the door, offer 30% below market value or asking price and walk out with the deal.

In my experience, and talking to other professional investors, this is far from the truth. Estate agents get loads of people walking in saying 'I am a professional investor. Can I have a good deal?' The reality is that if the agent is any good, they will already have a discrete client list of people who they have built relationships with over time.

In order to get estate agents' attention you will need to be professional, consistent and trustworthy. Never make an offer on a property if you do not intend to follow through. Stay in regular contact, go to viewings and talk to them about your strategies. Along with estate agents, Rightmove and local papers are great places to find potential properties. If you are looking near your own home, get to know your local properties, watch for houses that have been on the market a long while and look for run-down and empty properties.

The build team

Being professional, consistent and trustworthy also applies to working with builders – a good relationship is crucial. However, don't get complacent as you still need to check quotes. In an ideal situation, you would develop a niche and a model that you keep repeating. Once you achieve this, you can effectively keep a build team permanently busy. This ensures their success and loyalty, and guarantees the quality of your product.

Whether you are planning to buy and renovate a property, to keep it or sell it, you will need a good team you can rely on. You must understand the appropriate standard needed to rent a property. This can vary depending on the market you are targeting. Estate agents and letting agents are the best people to ask. Builders can also talk to you about refurbishment standards, but beware as in the early days, they may tell you what suits them in terms of how much they can charge you! Even when you have an established relationship with your builders, kitchen companies and other trades people and suppliers, you should regularly check their prices are remaining competitive. Treat them well, pay them promptly and build a trusting relationship so you know you can rely on them. It is not always about going for the cheapest option, it is about achieving the best.

If you have found the right run-down house, the rough diamond in the area that with a bit of polish and tender loving care you can turn into a gem, that is a great start. You have a tried and tested team or one recommended to you. Now you need to be clear about how you will fund and ultimately release those funds.

Rightmove is a well-known website that advertises property for sale or rent. It can be used to assess valuations and rentals. It is also possible to make assumptions about supply and demand in an area, along with other sites like Nethouse Price, MousePrice and Zoopla.

Case study 1

Fit for purpose

One really important thing to remember is that you are refurbishing your investment property for a purpose – for a specific tenant. Therefore, the work needs to result in a property that meets their tastes not yours. Valley was our first solo property within our joint venture partnership. Over the space of four days we managed to do more damage to the house and we delayed the rental of the property by a week, because we had to finish our unnecessary renovations.

What did we do? Well, the biggest and most costly mistake was to have not asked the letting agent what he thought we needed to do (as it was our first investment in a new area). Had we asked, he would have said, 'Add two cupboards in the kitchen and stop.'

What we did was take down the flowery border at the top of the walls in every room and, therefore, damaged the paintwork resulting in the redecoration of every room. We moved the sink in the bathroom from in front of the window to along the wall, which meant we also had to relocate the radiator, which in turn, meant lifting the carpet and floor boards!

Case study 1 (cont...)

This meant we had to buy fixtures and fittings, new bathroom flooring and, oh, we decided we didn't like the colour of the bathroom tiles – more expense!

Case study 2

Cashflow, capital and equity

A property I bought in 2013 needed a lot of work. It was damp and the back half of the kitchen ceiling was falling in. Sadly the previous tenants had been forced to live in these conditions, up to the point that I bought it. The deal was as follows:

Purchase price: £98,000

Loan at 75%: £73,500

Cost of works: £17,500
(This included a new roof, kitchen, four bathrooms, damp course, full redecoration, and carpets plus other minor repairs.)

So the cost to buy, hold and furnish through to letting was £10,000 approx.

Total spent in cash:

Deposit: £24,500

Repairs and costs: £27,500

Total: £52,000

Total cost of house purchase price plus repairs and buy costs
£98,000 + £27,500 = £125,500

New valuation: £145,000

The cashflow is gross £1,600 pcm.

Case study 2 (cont...)

After letting agent, mortgage, insurance and a 10% allowance for voids this comes to £750 approximately per month.

£750 x 12 months = £9,000 per year divided by the £52,000 cash invested in the deal = 17% return on investment.

When we remortgage to £145,000 (if we decide that is appropriate) the new loan will be £108,750 costing an extra £150 per month.

After we clear the existing mortgage that leaves £35,250.

Take away the £52,000 already spent and that leaves only £16,750 cash in the deal.

The new cashflow is still £600 after allowances and the new ROI is now 43% with 25% equity.

This deal was not bought 25% below market value, nor was it full remortgaged to take all the money back out. It is safe, cash flowing and still with genuine equity.

Knowing the numbers

When I buy a property I aim to get 50% of my cash back out, because I combine my investment technique with my (using other people's money) finance strategy. This means that I am focused on cashflow, getting as much as possible as quickly as possible. I am a preferred landlord by tenants in my area. I aim to provide a decent home, warm, dry and damp free that meets the living demands of my target tenant.

I now tend to fully renovate a property to a medium-high standard from day one. In my area this would incur £20,000–£25,000 upfront costs. And it also means that the property will not start generating rent until the work is completed – potentially three to four months down the line. Meanwhile, I have to pay the mortgage. A word of caution here: one person I spoke to invested in my area; bought in a postcode I would not touch and renovated over three months to a professional standard and created an HMO (house in multiple occupation). HMOs in the north west were frequently properties for single, unemployed men with multiple issues such as alcohol, drugs or mental health issues. Professionals want access to work and transport. So, the wrong property, in the wrong location and wrong refurbishment level means no cashflow and no leverage.

Now, 4–6 years of recession has created a change in the nature of the homeless population. They are not people on the fringe of society with multiple issues any longer, homeless people include families, repossessed former homeowners, soldiers – some vulnerable after time in service in the armed forces – and young people.

For years I said I would not rent to homeless tenants in the north west, nor would I pursue an HMO strategy. In 2014 we are piloting a new strategy on our own portfolio, renovating our stock to HMO standards so that we can rent to a charity that is housing the homeless.

Using Other People's Money 4th edition – once written – will let you know how well this strategy has worked. The plan is to double the rental income and triple the profit as voids, non-payment of rent and maintenance issues are all significantly reduced from the current benefit tenants.

So think of the tenant as your customer, with specific living requirements and possible rent restrictions like costs or accessibility and tailor your product (property) to meet that need.

In other areas we target working people that cannot afford their own flat close to town, so have to rent in a shared house. What is their worst fear? Dirty sharers! So we provide cleaners and private bathrooms.

Getting the money back out

At present, the lenders are taking the view that a property bought and sold in under six months is obviously suspicious and many will not lend to the buyer (or remortgagor). There is no point in listing which companies will or will not currently lend to you in under that time and what their conditions are, because it changes so frequently.

The general principle is this – you will need two lenders; you will buy the house through one lender (or bridge, through family or formal approaches) and then remortgage with a second lender. This is so that you can get a different surveyor to visit the property after you have renovated it and let them see it with new and clear eyes. Now, as the HBOS group seems to own most of the marketplace, you will need to plan this carefully. Know your lender and know their surveyors!

The other thing to consider is that each mortgage comes with conditions and often with 'tie-in' periods. You will need to get an initial mortgage or loan with no 'early redemption penalties'. This is why a commercial loan is a perfect example. If you look hard and wide enough, you will find building societies that also have no tie-ins. However, they may also only lend 60 or 65% of the purchase price. There is always a trade-off to be made.

You would then look for a second lender who is well placed in the market with a combination of high LTV and lower interest rates and fees. Now the lender you choose to be your second and permanent lender may change their rates, their conditions and all sorts of other things before you get a chance to complete – so you will need to watch the market and be flexible. Remember to evaluate the cost of the fees as well as the interest rates – your broker will help you.

For the last few years, one lender has been offering a 'light refurbishment product'; you will need a mortgage broker to access this lending. Make sure you understand the numbers and the pros and cons of this product.

You must know when you are working on a rough diamond that needs a full renovation and when you are buying a property that simply needs a partial refurbishment. Overall, remember that any money you invest must give you a return on that investment and that you are aiming to create a property that appeals to your prospective tenant or buyer, not yourself.

Consequences of this investment technique

From the point of offer we incur costs:

- The broker – £550–£750
- Survey – £350–£500
- Lender administration – £200 upwards
- Solicitor deposit – £400 towards a £1,500 total

At completion the mortgage becomes payable and there is still no income from the property or wages for you as an investor.

- Mortgage – £300–£450 pcm
- Insurance – £180–£250 up front

- Utility bills and council tax
- Builder fees – £7,500–£25,000 depending on the project

Once all the works are completed you then have to pay for: gas certificates, electrical certificates, possibly an HMO licence (local rules and fees apply), letting agent find fees and still the mortgage and the bills.

There is a long period where the project eats cash; this needs close management but more importantly adherence to a clear costed plan.

What about your time costs, everyone else is getting paid. How do you make a living – a return on your time? What is your time worth? How much actual time did the project take?

What is your time worth?

I estimate that it takes about ten days of my time to find, fix and fill a property. Sometimes it is less and other times a little longer if a project is complex.

From the point of offer to completion my quickest completion has been four weeks (I always survey and carry out searches). The longest has been ten weeks, which was caused by the homeowners needing to find a new property to enable them to move out.

From completion to being let, the projects have varied from seven days (for a quick window replacement and redecoration) to three months (for a full gutting to bare brick, rewire, plumb and full refit), which is three months of mortgage payments on one or possibly two properties, which you need to budget for – and, of course, include a contingency plan in case of overrun.

Long term consequences and risks

When I was in the process of buying one of my properties, between offer and completion two other properties on the street were repossessed and advertised on Rightmove for approximately £10,000–£15,000 lower than the ceiling price of the street. I cancelled my plans to 'refurb and flip' (Chapter 11) and just carried out a light redecorating and rented out the property. That is why you need to understand the risks and consequences and to have a fall-back plan.

What if the property in case study 2 had not reached the £145,000 revaluation estimate? Can you afford to leave cash in the deal – where did it come from and when must it be repaid?

Cost to establish, time implications and impact on lifestyle.

Now that we are moving into the meat of property investment techniques, there are genuine consequences on your time and lifestyle.

With buy and refurbish, the first consideration is where you invest and how far that is from your home. Do you work full or part-time? Do you have a family and can you afford or want to stay away over night in your area if needed.

You can see from the case studies above the potential time certain-sized projects take and the funds needed to complete the project. You also need to factor in the cost of petrol, food and accommodation.

I have an excellent team that I trust implicitly. I only visit my areas (the areas where I already own properties or where I am looking to buy properties) once or twice a month for 2–3 days at a time. This increases if we have a lot more projects on the go, but this is an average. Can you afford to be away from home, to cover the cost of petrol, hotel bills, food. What about the family you leave behind, do they understand? I think my family has a party every time I go away!

Lastly, how have you funded your life during this time and where are your daily funds coming from? What impact has running this project had on your lifestyle?

Chapter 11 Buying to sell – flipping

Buying to sell is an attractive strategy especially now with media promises of property price rises. Flipping enables you to put your money into a deal, pay for the refurbishment costs using an assortment of financial strategies, sell the completed project and then get the money invested plus a profit back out again.

However, buying to sell is a very special game in any market and I still believe this market is challenging. You will really need to understand your market, both as the buyer and as a seller of a 'ready-to-move-in' home. After all, you are selling to 'want-to-be' homeowners or 'ready-to-rent-out' investors.

This is a crucial distinction before you even buy a property to flip. Who is your target market? Like the point I raised in buy and hold (Chapter 10) about the tenant type and needs – new buyers' needs vary dramatically. Imagine the buying motivation of a first-time buyer compared to an investor.

While they may both be driven by price, the first-time buyer will look at the property through the emotional eye of a couple making a life together. The investor (should) be viewing the property through the hardened eyes of a business owner looking for a return on capital employed.

Focus on the end result and market accordingly. A large three-bedroom house with only a shower not a bath could mean that families with young children will be put off. There is a difference between preparing a house for an investor to buy as a business and a member of the general public looking for a home.

Tax implications

There are tax implications with this strategy as the sale produces a taxable profit – rather than cash released as debt through a remortgage which is tax free. While you can off-set this with your annual capital gains tax allowance, this is currently only £10,600 per person and once used is gone, it also can't be carried forward. This technique would work well if you have a large extended family who you trust. Otherwise, you will give up to 28% or more to the tax man. If you remortgage, the money released is tax-free debt!

If the cash released is immediately reinvested this can reduce the tax burden but you need to check your finance strategy with your accountant and tax advisors.

I have attempted this strategy twice with a poor result (thank goodness for my second exit strategy!). I personally feel the market is still too unpredictable and that means this is a high risk technique by my standards. Or maybe I mean the house prices are still relatively static and the surveyors too unpredictable.

If you decide to pursue this strategy, there are lots of ways that you can finance a deal like this. For example, using bridging finance (from family and friends, or a bridging specialist) to purchase the property, either outright or with a mortgage to cover 75%. Then use credit cards to do the refurbishment or maybe make an agreement with the builder to pay them at the sale of the property to cover the rest of the costs.

You can see already how this can be a more complex type of project using a blend of finance strategies. Of course, the investment strategy itself must be absolutely solid!

Making it work – worst house in the best street

The most crucial aspect of making this strategy work is:

- finding the right property,
- getting your budget right,
- managing your team,
- perfecting your marketing.

Finding the right property is easy if you think of it this way: you want to find the worst house in the best street. This means that you can buy undervalue, add value (within a tightly controlled budget) and then sell at just under the ceiling price. Remember, every street will have a ceiling price and deciding to buck the trend will be more difficult than you imagine.

If you are going to make this work, then you really need to make sure that you keep an eye on the timescales for your refurbishment so that your costs don't run too high. Budget properly for the tools and help needed for the refurbishment, as a mistake here will cost you your profit.

There is a risk that the refurbishment will take longer than you plan, especially with older properties. If your project overruns, it will eat into your profit, factor in an overrun to your costs. Most importantly, you will need to make sure that you can cover the cashflow required to cover the monthly costs whilst you are waiting for work to finish or the sale to go through. This is particularly important if you use bridging finance (Chapter 7). A deal that slips into another month of bridging costs could cost you another £1,500 extra in bridging costs!

Making every penny count – manage your emotions, your team and your budget

The temptation with a property is to get emotionally involved in the deal – 'It's a lovely house'. No, it's not. It's a great business opportunity as long as you can stick to your plan. You will need to be sure that any refurbishment work or improvements that you carry out are actually going to add value to the house. Don't go in and change things that don't necessarily need changing just because it is not to your taste. Kerb appeal is obviously something to think about, but once inside the house you need to know how much extra value adding another bathroom would bring.

The kitchen is always important – it needs to have enough room to move, enough cupboard space to store things, and be clean and tidy. The same considerations need to be applied to the bathroom. A neat trick for quick bathroom refurbishment is to re-mastic round the bath and the sink, replace the taps and then thoroughly clean. It is not always necessary to replace a bath suite – unless of course it is not white! Does it matter if the bathroom is downstairs or is that the norm for the area? Remember to tailor your product to your customer's taste, not yours!

Over cautious and pleasantly surprised

What do I mean by this? When undertaking a project like this, I carry out research to demonstrate the 'weakest' value of the property while also knowing the 'reasonable' potential sale price. By that I mean, never base your profit figures on the maximum sale prices in the area when calculating your figures.

You will also need to consider how much profit you want to make on a deal to make it worthwhile. Some people are happy to do deals for £10,000. Other investors would not look at a deal unless there was at least £50,000–£100,000 profit in the project or a significant return (75–100%) on capital employed after all the costs.

So be overly cautious on your profit projections and then pleasantly surprised at an increased profit outcome, rather than horrified at a weak profit margin. Make allowances in terms of time (and cash) to cover the refurbishment and sale. For example, add a contingency budget of eight weeks – just in case. Also add between 10–20% contingency and overrun on the refurbishment costs (dependent on the size of the project). It is far better in my opinion to only expect £20,000 profit and then make £30,000, than to expect £30,000 but only make £20,000.

Be realistic

I recently worked out two property buy and sell examples for a talk I was giving. In the first example, the property value was approximately £100,000 and I used £20,000 as the refurbishment budget. In total the project needed £55,000 cash (plus 75% loan) to refurbish, pay the mortgage or loan during works and then resell. Using current reports of property price indices, I managed to increase the value (on paper) through inflation and refurbishment to £124,000. That meant the project lost £6,000 and cost me 40 days of time to project manage. Not a good risk!

By taking a property value of £250,000 and spending the same amount of time – but with a slightly higher refurbishment budget of £27,500 – the cost to fund the project jumps to £106,000 (higher fees and a larger deposit playing their respective parts). In the end, again using published property prices increases, the value moved to £312,500 and yes there was just under £19,000 profit. But the project took ten months and more than forty days – that is just £475 wages per day. This strategy needs careful consideration.

For some of you, £19,000 is worth risking £106,000 cash – I do not believe that is a good enough return. Why? Well if you borrowed £106,000 through family (it's cheaper than bridging remember) then at just 5% for 10 months it would have cost you another £4,416 now putting you at £14,584 potential profit. There is just not enough return given the risk. This starts to be a gamble. Use your own cash and maybe you will be comfortable with the risk. Using bridging or other people's money and I am not convinced.

Marketing – what's the plan?

Think about how you are going to market the property. Will it be marketed with empty rooms or will it be marketed with furniture? How will the property be advertised? Will you be advertising it yourself, will you go through newspapers or websites or place it with an estate agent?

At what point in the refurbishment process can someone come and see the property? I bought a house where I saw it before the builder started work, and then saw it again while works were being carried out. Maybe you could enable the future homeowner to choose the colour scheme?

If you have bought the property through an estate agent, then why not stay in touch and offer them the new sale as part of your relationship-building strategy? You can then use the expertise of the local estate agent to guide and influence some of your refurbishment decisions.

On a new deal bought direct from the home owner, I asked my local estate agent to view the property and give me their opinion of essential works needed to ensure a quick sale. Then I invited the builder round to give me their opinion on the essential works needed to sell the house quickly to a specific target market. I made a judgement where the two lists differed – based on the cost of works and the potential return. Builders and estate agents will expect to get the business if the deal goes through. Think carefully about how you use their time and respect their businesses.

I would still advertise a property on websites and newspapers just to speed the selling process and maximise the rate of return of the initial money invested. Like any of the strategies I have talked about so far, you need to understand both the market you are operating in and the clients/tenants/buyers or investors that will finally take possession of the property.

Case study

Redeveloping to order

I worked with a mentee to see how they could maximise the income from their portfolio. They were in a good position in terms of gearing – the overall portfolio was at 75%. They wanted to see how they could raise more cash to continue investing.

My first questions as part of our initial strategy session were: how much cashflow did they have as a target; and where was the portfolio in terms of meeting that financially-free target figure?

As we examined strategies for each property and various combinations, it became clear they had one property that could be redeveloped. The challenge was they did not have the funds to pay for the work.

The property was in a highly desirable street. I set a list of research questions: was there a market (need) for the planned redevelopment?

Would planning permission be granted? Once we knew there was a potential market and the project was feasible, we moved on to the costs involved: what would the potential resale value be (remember to under estimate)? What were the build costs? What were the solicitor and estate agent fees?

This project became a development deal where the seller could influence the interior design of the finished project. How? They effectively bought the finished property through an exchange with delayed completion.

The buyer paid a deposit of 14% upfront (more than the usual 10%), which funded the cost of the redevelopment.

The final deal meant an uplift in value of £150,000 for a cost of £50,000 funded by the new owner. The profit is £100,000 plus the equity already in the property. The next phase of the plan was to invest in more cashflowing properties as that is the primary target. Expected cashflow increase to be over £1,000 pcm and counting.

Consequences – best time and lost time

Your budget and, therefore, profit will be based on a timescale (as mentioned previously). You must budget for overruns, as well as for extra interest costs and/or extra refurbishment costs. If the overall aim of this strategy is to buy at a discount and then make a profit, you need to know that every penny you spend will add value. I roughly calculate that the refurbishment work I am doing will mean each pound spent will generate at least £3 pounds of extra capital value, maybe £2–2.50 per pound spent on larger deals.

Finally, think about the economic environment. We all know that there are more popular times of the year to buy, everyone loves to buy when the sun is out. Look at your timescales and maybe rethink your plans if the timescale means that you will be going to market just after Christmas.

Speak to the estate agents about peak buying times in your area and work to that timescale. Above all, if you are planning to resell choose your property with your buyer in mind. See if you can find the potential buyer before you complete on your deal, therefore all refurbishment work would in effect be carried out to order, especially if they sign a contract stating that.

Think about the case study on page 79 (Cashflow, capital and equity) we spent £17,500 on the refurb and increased the value by £47,000. We had a target of £125,000 as a final conservative valuation. Cautious figures lead to a pleasant surprise – this is a much happier way round.

Time and cash implications in a buy-to-sell strategy are high. The level of refurbishment can be high and take time. The cost of refurbishment, mortgage and loan repayments can be stressful if not managed properly. Above all, you must be committed and focused to make this strategy a success. That means this strategy impacts on your life and the life of your family!

Chapter 12 Auctions, developing and HMOs

I don't go to auctions to buy property myself; I get too excited and have to sit on my hands in case I accidentally buy anything by mistake.

Auctions definitely need a health warning – the environment and the job of the auctioneer is to create drama and excitement around each 'lot' or property for sale.

The property will be advertised with a guide price, this means nothing. It is just a number to start bidding from or ignore. The auctioneer will advise a seller on a guide price, but like any sale ticket it is designed to catch your eye. The reserve price is key and this is set by the seller, again in consultation with the auctioneer. This is the minimum price that the seller will accept and hence why it is kept secret from the buyers in the room.

The auctioneers must get bidding above the reserve price before they can bring the hammer down to complete on a sale.

The auctioneer may create interest by taking bids 'off the wall'. This is a technique designed to drive interest and may not actually be a bid from a real person. Theoretically if your bid is below the reserve the auctioneer might take a bid off the wall to encourage you to raise your offer until you reach the reserve. They are not allowed to then force the sale price higher, once reserve is reached no more off the wall bids are allowed to be taken – or created.

The bidding process is designed to be quick, to drive emotion and keep energy high in the hope that you bid more than you planned – so beware.

You can of course offer a bid before auction and if the seller agrees the property can be sold before anyone enters the room. Equally if a property is not sold in the room you can make the auctioneer an offer which the seller may accept.

Have a budget – read the contract

You must be prepared:

1. View the property – never buy what you have not seen. I once saw a mid-terraced house that had a tree growing through the kitchen – the front looked perfectly normal.

2. Check the contract – watch for clauses and conditions limiting the sale or use, or stipulating conditions attached to completion. Again we viewed a property which had a lovely spiral staircase – upon further checks it was obvious that it was listed and could not be changed in any way.

3. Run the numbers and add a large contingency on top of a normal consideration – beware of auction fees and the need for speed. While most properties complete in the normal 28 days, some sellers apply additional conditions to their properties and they must be met or there are significant penalties.

4. When the hammer falls that is in effect exchange and you will need to pay the 10% deposit and sign the contract – now you can see what Kevin Wright was talking about in his top tips in Chapter 7.

One of our portfolio services includes buying properties at auction. We buy them for approximately £40–50,000 with an estimated £20–30,000 refurbishment budget. Over the next three months the properties are completely turned around, the property gutted and then fully reconditioned. We then have a contract in place to house vulnerable tenants through a government lease, some of which offer guaranteed rent until 2019.

The majority of properties we redevelop and recondition are changed over to HMO or multi-let status. We target the properties to fall just under the local regulations for HMO status and licencing.

These properties and the HMO strategy are much more involved and demanding than a normal buy-to-let, but in return they offer a much higher rental income. I am currently converting two properties:

1. A four bed house needing £8,000 of work which will increase the rental income from £695 per month to £880, which will be a 27.75% return on the £8,000 budget in the first year.

2. A three bed house needing £15,000 of work which will increase the rent from £450 to £880 per month, this will be a 34.4% ROI on our cash.

On top of the increased rental profit the letting agent fees have been reduced to 8% from 10% and voids are expected to be nil as there is a waiting list for this type of housing. Lastly I expect the maintenance to be dramatically reduced on this contract as the tenants have a great deal more support and inspection. So hopefully that will be another combined 10–12% income from saved costs.

Management is key

Like all deals, management of the process is crucial, from the buying phase (auctions require speed and cash as a mortgage takes too long) to the refurbishing phase; again pay attention to time as time costs money and budgets, which risks profits.

Then, of course, there is the management of the tenants as no rental income means no profit at all.

Time implications

Buying at auction is definitely a quicker process than buying direct or through an estate agent as completion will take place in 28 days or less. This can save a month or two of costs on money released through remortgage and not employed and earning interest. But it requires the full purchase price and cost of works to be funded through cash as the time savings are also a restriction to getting a mortgage.

Emotion verses spreadsheet

This is a riskier way to buy unless you view it, research it, work it out, and if someone bids over your budget – let them have it!

Know your exit strategy in advance whether its buy and hold or buy and flip – then follow the tips in the previous two chapters. Use your deal analyser!

Consequences and impact on time, finances and lifestyle

As with any project involving the development or refurbishment of a property you need to understand how you are going to fund the project, and how you are going to pay the cost of funding the project. Then how will you earn money – how much and when? You can see the implications will largely come from the strategy you employ after the auction process is completed.

The consequences with this buying technique (other than funding issues) lie in the timing of auctions. They are not daily. There is a temptation, especially with the added emotion of the the auction, to become a desperate buyer. Beware.

And, of course, auctions are not necessarily held in your town or your investment area, so this requires planning, nerves of steel and the ability to travel (for viewings at set times and the auction itself). While you can bid online or by phone, it is better to be present and see the competition.

Lastly the impact on your lifestyle ... the strategy again will influence this, but generally expect this project to be all-consuming and time-intensive. This is not an easy strategy for those with a regular nine-to-five job.

Chapter 13 Splitting

Freehold-leasehold: the parts are greater than the sum. What makes this strategy so clever?

By buying a property that is actually just a 'lump' of flats you can generate a lot of cash-generating exit strategies. First, for example, you could keep all the flats and make even more cashflow. Or you could sell one or two flats and have both the benefit of cashflow and future capital appreciation from those you keep while generating some immediate cash lump sums from those you sell. Or you could sell some of the flats and just keep one flat for yourself for free.

This is only made possible if you get your power team and your numbers right. The variations and opportunities are endless and highly profitable if you:

- find the right deal,
- have an expert solicitor and experienced broker,
- get the seller on side,
- build up a rapport with a local letting agent with experience,
- have a great deal of nerve.

Above all, it is about understanding the strategy, working out the combination of funding structures and knowing where and how the money will be made in the deal.

Freehold-leasehold?

'Freehold-leasehold' is a common commercial strategy often seen when there are flats above a shop. Let's start with the term 'freehold' – this is the term for the title of a property. In other words, the Queen who owns England gives you permission to build on her land without additional charges. So you own the free holding of the land and the properties on it.

'Leasehold' means that you own only the bricks and mortar and you effectively are renting or leasing the land from the freeholder. In return, they charge you rent (usually something small like £100 per annum; in the old days a peppercorn was used, hence the term 'peppercorn rent').

Houses can be leasehold properties and the freeholder in the case of a single dwelling will simply charge the ground rent and that is all. In the case of a multiple dwelling, like flats, the freeholder will have responsibilities to maintain the exterior of the building and all the common areas. They will pass the cost of ongoing maintenance on to you and will also invoice you for the time taken to handle the management of the building through an additional service charge.

What does a freehold-leasehold look like?

A typical property would be a Victorian townhouse that had been converted into flats many years ago. It could also look like an ordinary house. It is very unlikely to be new build or a bungalow.

It must have an 'established use' meaning that the flats have been in existence long enough that the utility companies and post office recognise them as separate entities. Of course, the whole building must be for sale; otherwise you are just buying a few flats. So there is this contradiction between the building being considered as one entity, just one property as far as land registry is concerned, and the component flats which have been in practical use for so long that the utility companies see the building as separate flats.

Listings for this type of building can be found at auctions, with estate agents or on Rightmove. It is a more complex purchase, often involving the purchase of three or more component flats at the same time. You will need to prepare, and a good idea may be to have a checklist of what to look out for. These include things like planning permission, which can be checked out with the local council in the early stages of your research. You will need to know whether planning permission to change the 'house' into flats was obtained and, if so, how long ago.

Next, you will need to know if each unit or flat has its own front door, gas and electricity supply, kitchen, bathroom/toilet and bedroom. The property must be a recognisable flat in itself – a separate dwelling in its own right. If not, you will have to install this and that will mean a full renovation budget.

Getting the team right

Unlike previous chapters where it was the builder who was so important, in this strategy you need to have an experienced solicitor who understands and has dealt with this type of purchase before. The solicitor will need to be experienced in splitting the freehold into leases. You will also need an accountant or go online and set up a Limited Company, and at some point you will be trading these properties, which means you'll need an experienced broker or commercial mortgage arrangement, plus, of course, an architect to draw the plans.

Your broker will need to know which lenders are happy to lend on this type of deal. Make sure you fully describe the property to the broker, forgetting to mention that a property has two kitchens can break the mortgage offer at the point of survey and cause untold stress. This sort of problem is not insurmountable but needs to be clearly placed on the table for discussing and planning!

In this model you will be creating new leases and essentially buying newly leased properties and some lenders don't like that at the moment. The deal falls into the six-month trap as the new lease and the purchase from the Limited Company essentially mean that the property will not have been owned by the immediate seller for six months. You will also need to have a number of different lenders involved because no one lender will want to feel overexposed by lending on the whole property.

So, for example, in a property consisting of four established flats you will need to find four lenders who are prepared to lend on newly created leases! You may need to ask family or friends to hold the mortgages for you.

Getting the seller and occupiers on side

Then, of course, you really need to consider the seller as part of your team because they have the power to enable the deal or not. Each component part or flat will need to be visited at least three times; first by you, then by a mortgage surveyor and then by an architect who will draw the plans needed to create the leases. As you can imagine, this might inconvenience any tenants in the property, as they will need to either provide keys and give access permission or be present at every viewing. All the component parts will need to be viewed.

You will also need to make sure that the mortgage surveyors do not meet or hear about the architect and, therefore, preferably not meet the tenants either. The mortgage surveyor just needs to value the flats and not worry about the future creation of leases. This whole process can cause major time delays and your seller will need to understand this is not going to be the world's quickest purchasing system.

Making the numbers work – part 1

As with all investment deals, it is important to do your research on your target property and make sure the numbers work out in your favour (i.e. profitably) before viewing at all. When we talk about the figures involved in these deals, it is slightly different from a regular buy-to-let investment.

You are looking for a property where 75% of the final value of the component flats (because you will get a 75% LTV mortgage for example) equals or exceeds the cost of the original freehold property purchase price, the buying costs (solicitors, surveys, etc.) and the cost of any building or refurbishment works needed. If this works, then you will have found yourself the ultimate deal.

Let me go over these numbers again.

Let's pick an easy example. The freehold property is worth £300,000 (and you pay the asking price just to make it easy). The house was split into four self-contained one-bedroom flats about 15 years ago. A separate one-bedroom flat is easily worth £100,000.

See how easy I am making the maths? It really does not work out quite so simply in real life, but hopefully you will get the point of the strategy and then explore for yourself.

So when you split the title into four separate one-bedroom flats and get four separate mortgages at 75% LTV – you will have a mortgage 'cash pot' of 4 x £75,000 which equals £300,000, the cost of the purchase price.

Now, if you get a better purchase price or better valuations on the final flats, then you will also get enough money through on the mortgages to cover the purchase costs and maybe any renovations required.

Let me do another example with slightly different figures to help you understand further.

Making the numbers work – part 2

In the example in the diagram on the next page you will see that the freehold property is being sold for £300,000. Once you have built up a rapport with the estate agent, you will be able to negotiate confidently in the knowledge that there will be plenty of viewings but not many offers, as few investors know how to make this type of deal work.

You will be able to calculate the value of the leasehold units through plenty of research. Always assume the lowest component values to be extra cautious. Again, speak to your broker and know what loans and LTVs you can get on all four flats (in this example).

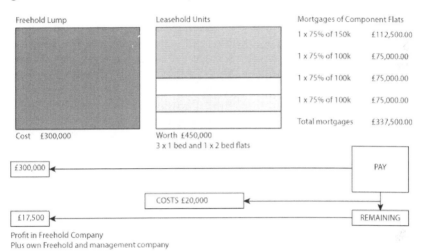

Freehold Lump	Leasehold Units	Mortgages of Component Flats	
		1 x 75% of 150k	£112,500.00
		1 x 75% of 100k	£75,000.00
		1 x 75% of 100k	£75,000.00
		1 x 75% of 100k	£75,000.00
		Total mortgages	£337,500.00
Cost £300,000	Worth £450,000 3 x 1 bed and 1 x 2 bed flats		

£300,000 ← PAY

COSTS £20,000 ←

£17,500 ← REMAINING

Profit in Freehold Company
Plus own Freehold and management company

If you buy the place for £275,000 and get valuations on the three one-bedroom flats at £120,000 each, then your profit could soar to £87,500 instead of just £17,500.

On the gloomy side, if the mortgage on the two-bedroom flat comes in at 70% LTV (giving a mortgage of £105,000) and your cost calculations were wrong meaning you need to spend £40,000 instead of £20,000, then you would have to put £10,000 in the deal or sell one or more of the flats.

Knowing the numbers inside and out is critical to the success of this strategy and that is why cautious valuations on your part are an absolute must.

However, if the deal did end up costing you £10,000 of your cash (providing you could access the funds), that would work out as £2,500 per flat which is still a bargain. Some investors will use this strategy even if they do have to put money in the deal because it can be a very cheap way of acquiring flats and, therefore, cashflow.

Time and life consequences

This technique takes a lot of time, research and understanding before you even put in an offer. A bit like lease options in Chapter 15 there are strategic development costs in time spent to understand the technique, which do not necessarily earn you any income. If you can afford to learn and develop this technique then it could be worth investing your time.

Unlike lease options, in my opinion, for the determined math-savvy investor this is a great portfolio building strategy. You use your cash to buy and split, remortgage or sell and go again. How much time and money can you afford to invest to make this technique work for you?

This strategy will take a lot of time, and unless you are very lucky, it will require a lot of travelling to find your target area. Not everyone has this style of property on their doorstep! During the deals pressure on your time and nerves will be intense, and as I had mentioned previously, you really need to get the investor on your side and have the cooperation of the tenants to make this work.

If you learn the technique and then can afford to fund the pre-purchase costs of making a deal happen then the return on both time and money will be worth it. Remember there may be a number of properties that never make it to completion but that do cost you survey fees, solicitor fees and broker fees.

Go into this with your eyes open.

Chapter 14 Rent to rent

In its most basic form, this strategy involves leasing a large, three or more bedroom, property and then, with the owner's full consent, sub-leasing the rooms. This can be carried out through a contract directly with the owners or via a letting agent. The best contract to use for this form of letting is a specialist management contract.

As with everything in life, there are a number of other considerations you must adhere to, and major pitfalls to avoid if you are to set things up correctly, legally and safely. Using the correct contract is a must – trying to edit and alter an AST to fit is like walking into a legal minefield. You must ensure the correct mortgage product is in place, and both you and the landlord have adequate insurance. It is also crucial to ensure you have an exit strategy – what happens when you want to hand the property back?

This strategy can solve the landlord's problems; can give the agents less work while still getting paid (by the landlord) and can very quickly (as fast as 3 days!) create a positive cashflow for you. A true win for all parties involved.

- Find a landlord who is fed up, tired, bored or lives a long distance away from the property and offer to help.
- You need to find these deals in your area, within a 30 minutes' drive.
- Negotiate terms to lease their property for 3+ years.
- Create a desirable home where young professionals will want to live.

Ideally, you would be looking to take control of an existing HMO as this will minimise your financial input – it will already have fire doors, fire alarms etc. Unlike lease options, you will have no solicitor fees and refurbishment costs can be as low as £450!

You will be working in partnership with the current owner, who has often self-managed the property for years and has lost interest, become ill, old or just tired of tenants. In the long run, you might find that the landlord agrees to sell – that may be a bonus. The downside is that implementing this strategy will result in you taking on the role of a specialist letting agent, but it can be and has been done very successfully whilst in full-time employment.

You need to find these deals in your area. This is not a long distance technique!

I worked with a coaching client who effectively operated this strategy by luck rather than judgement. They knew an investor who lived a long way from a small portfolio of properties. The landlord and investor agreed a profit level that the landlord wanted – it was then up to the investor to maximise the rental income and benefit from any remaining profit. They effectively acted as a letting agent.

Be careful, as with all deals, to make sure that it stacks up for you. What resource does a deal need? Your time, which is finite and valuable? Your knowledge, which is abundant and a replenishable resource to be leveraged? Or your money, which again I would suggest is finite and valuable but can also be leveraged? Then decide on the value of using or risking those resources and make sure you charge or earn accordingly.

Think what you want to earn and understand the value of your time as an hourly rate. For example if you want to take home £3,000 per month from managing rental properties using rent to rent, think how many days a week can you work on this project (once you have found the properties). You might have a job or be doing other property deals – you need to understand your capacity.

Let's assume you can spend ten hours per week – you will need to be available 52 weeks of the year – that's a total of 520 hours to earn £36,000 after tax and costs.

What are the business costs of this rent to rent technique? Phone calls, emails, travel costs to visit the properties, professional insurance, book keeping and accounts – most importantly advertising costs to advertise the vacant rooms to tenants. That's an initial budget of £10,000 plus of course tax and national insurance – you will need to monitor and adjust this figure.

So you will need to earn about £60,000 in your 520 hours of time available, which is an hourly rate of £115.40, let's make it £120 to make the maths nice. Now you can see that every 15 minute slot is £30.

You will need to think about the income-saving, income-generating and income-speculating time model I explained on page 10 of Chapter 1 the Business of Investing. You will need to manage your time because this model assumes that you will be earning every moment of your 520 hours and that is not possible with admin and marketing tasks to be completed.

Think carefully. If you make £120 profit per room after the rent, insurance and other costs are deducted, then you can only afford to spend one hour of your time that month to take care of that tenant. In a six month period if that tenant's arrival (itinerary and check in), ongoing rent payment checks (monthly) and final check out (exit meeting, room clean and marketing to re-let) all take less than six hours of work – you will have a profitable business. So that means the better your systems and advertising the more money you will earn for less time.

Now multiply that by four rooms and you need each property to earn over £480 per month profit and take you less than 24 hours to manage in each six month period. You now have a business plan to put into action. And £3,000 per month net for ten hours work (if you can make this work) is an amazing salary!

What if you could maximise the rental income so that there was enough profit to pay someone else to be the letting agent – a perfectly sweet deal then!

Case study

The Multi-Let Cashflow System (MLCS)

As this strategy will effectively create a lettings business, you need to be clear about what works best for you in terms of area, property type and tenant type. Both LHA and student tenants can be quite demanding, so focusing on young professionals whom you 'train' to call your build team with problems will make this strategy a lot less time intensive!

My good friend, Francis Dolley, and his daughter Emily have made this strategy an art form and shared an example with me so you can see how the numbers work. They operate in Bristol and work with professional tenants.

Now, remember, you are essentially renting the property from a letting agent or landlord. So to acquire (let) an average property in Bristol would need the first month's rent and a deposit of £2,000. The letting agent fees are around £400 and average refurbishment costs are £750.

So what are the pitfalls of this strategy?

People often ask, 'What if the primary landlord asks for the property back after the initial term?' Normally the 'tired' landlords who willingly agree to this type of strategy are feeing some pain – empty rooms, missing rent – and either don't seem to care or do not know what to do about it. This strategy is the answer to their prayers, offering them guaranteed rent with no voids and no hassle. In London, this place in the market is taken by the council and housing association schemes.

Francis and Emily found that most of their landlords live out of the area and are obviously only interested in receiving the monthly rent. Even if the landlord did take the property back after 12 months, you would still have made an excellent return on your investment. If the landlord terminated the agreement, you would of course remove all the items that made the property more desirable and you would no longer be managing the property, which would put the landlord right back where he started.

Most landlords would be smart enough to recognise this, but it does happen. I have just been speaking with a former rent to rent property business owner whom we are going to start mentoring to create a new sourcing business, after their portfolio of rent to rent properties was reclaimed by the respective landlords to sell. In one month their whole business model collapsed.

As Francis commented, 'We have had only one landlord out of nine ask for their property back and this was due to illness. We always pay the rent on time, we look after the properties and we don't bother the landlord with constant problems. Why would they want to go back to empty rooms and unpaid rent?'

'There is a risk that you may not be able to rent the rooms.' Emily added, 'You must fully research your target area and tenants both on and offline to ensure that there is a demand for the rooms – we have a totally systemised process for this. We had one underperforming property with a small and difficult room to let. We decided to drop the rent to well below market value to prevent voids and did not renew this contract.' Another significant factor to consider is what happens if it all goes wrong? You have a commitment and a contract with your tenants?

Emily and Francis explained two worst case scenarios:

1. If the landlord is declared bankrupt and a repossession order is issued, the tenant (you) can apply to the courts to postpone the date for two months and then issue your tenants with notice to quit. The court may make a further postponement if you can arrange payments directly to the mortgage company. On the plus side, the landlord could well become a seller, which could be an opportunity for you to purchase the property.

2. What if the landlord dies? The responsibilities of the landlord will be transferred to the new owner of the property. In the first instance, this will be the executor, and then it will be whoever the property is sold or transferred to. The bank accounts belonging to the deceased may be frozen. If this is the case, you should keep the money safe and forward it to the new landlord as soon as you get the details. Family members of the deceased landlord may try and convince you to pay rent to them, but it could be that they may not be legally entitled to it. The new owners may wish to sell the property fast, which, again, could be a great opportunity for you.

Article 4 – the legal bit

You will need to keep up to date with the constantly changing legislation, such as Article 4. In the past, Article 4 Directions were issued by local councils in circumstances where specific control over development was required, primarily where the character of an area of acknowledged importance would be threatened.

They were more commonly applied to conservation areas. Councils have now extended Article 4 in some cases to entire cities. Commentators have referred to this as the de-studentification of entire areas. This does not necessarily affect the rent to rent if you follow some straightforward guidelines. You will need to check with your council to see if Article 4 has been implemented in your area.

What makes this a good strategy? Well, personally, I think this strategy says what it does on the tin – it's simple and straightforward and a route to income – providing you can organise and plan it properly.

The main benefits of using this strategy are:

- It limits exposure to interest rates, as the lease fees are fixed, giving a reliable long-term cashflow.
- It lets you integrate the management of your existing portfolio and gives you the economy of scale to grow your business.
- A massive return on investment – Francis and family make on average £745 per property for an average of £3,500 cash input – that's 2,554% ROI!
- It's a sensible model – find a property, get it rented and get the cashflow – there is no delay for surveys, brokers or mortgage offers. Francis' fastest deal was three days from initial viewing to cashflow!

Critical success factors:

- A targeted area with well-managed relationships with local letting agents.
- Clear strategy on property and tenant type.
- Highly organised with good systems and structures in place.
- Know the relevant legislation – you have committed to pay the landlord!
- Reinvest the cashflow into buy-to-lets and HMOs of your own.

Consequences and time implications

This investment technique is designed to take a small amount of your time (depending on the size of the rent to rent portfolio you develop), however the time does need to be spread over 52 weeks of the year. You will need an excellent support team and good systems in place to minimise the impact on your personal life.

Having said that the process of working closely in one area means you will discover properties for sale. If you can either run this business alongside a full-time job or another property technique, rent to rent is one way to generate extra income that you can invest in deals for yourself. Of course you can also create a pot of money ready for when one of your landlords decides to retire.

With the right systems and a good team this is an excellent cashflowing business. Francis and Emily can help, they are great people to have on your team.

Chapter 15 Lease options

What is a lease option? This takes the rent to rent technique and effectively focuses on the option to buy as a way to get a property at a reduced price by agreeing your offer now and then buying later.

The fact is that this technique pivots on your ability to gamble on property prices. If the deal works then the lease holder has control of a property with no mortgage, potential cashflow (we'll come to that) and then the chance to make a 'fortune' when the property prices increase and they enact their option at a much lower price, as agreed.

The issues for me are:

1. Who is likely to agree to this sort of deal?

2. What are your rules to ensure this is a good deal, financially and in terms of your time?

3. What if property prices do not go up or don't rise until later than planned?

4. What if interest rates go up?

5. Or the seller dies before the deal is complete? Or they go bankrupt?

6. Is it really that easy?

Lease options explained

A lease option is an all-encompassing term. First, there is a long lease (three to seven years) and then there is an option to buy the property. You can use this option to 'buy' a property for your portfolio or to 'sell' the house on to a tenant buyer. A lease option is a way to take control of a property and its cashflow without having to take out a mortgage right now, but giving you the option of buying the property in the future at a price agreed today.

Let's start with the lease. A lease is a legal contract, which in this context is similar to an Assured Shorthold Tenancy (AST) in that it is a contract between two parties where one grants the other permission to stay in a property under certain conditions in exchange for a fee. A lease might grant a three-year stay for a monthly fee (rent) with the potential to give 30 days' notice to leave by either party. The difference with an AST is the assumption that you stay in the property. The lease assumes that you will re-rent the property to a third party.

A purchase option is another component of the contract and this separate document states that if conditions are met, the property can be bought for the agreed purchase price at any point between now and the fixed date in the future. It might also give the right to extend that purchase date.

So a lease option in the way we use the combined term means two contracts that give the holder the right to rent the property for a fixed period of time and the right, but not the obligation, to buy the property for a price agreed today, but to complete on the sale at a time agreed in the future.

So the advantages are that you control a house without having to have a mortgage – great idea if you have poor credit rating or no cash to invest just like rent to rent. My experience of spending six months in 2011 and £4,000 advertising for deals and coaching many other investors is that lease options are not as simple as many experts would have you believe. I also believe that the focus of the strategy is all wrong – out of balance. Let's go through it chronologically and you can form your opinion. As a caveat, I think you should definitely understand this strategy and use it if a deal is worth it but, personally, I do not think this makes sense as a sole and primary strategy in this market.

Rent to rent is much simpler and therefore easier to agree with a landlord. Plus of course rent to rent works with investors that understand business and property and not members of the public in a distressed state about a personal crisis.

The focus of any strategy

It has to be the cashflow. That for me is number one. If there is no significant cashflow, then there is no deal to be had. Why? Each deal comes with debt.

All right, in this example the debt is held by someone else, but there is a debt to be paid on the property regardless.

Once I know a deal will cashflow according to my rules (and I will run through those in a minute), then I want to know how 'easy' the deal is to arrange. I believe that with increasing complexity comes increased time costs and increased risk. Remember to cost out your hourly rate, if the deal is hard to explain you are not earning money!

Time costs refer to how long it will take compared to other strategies to get a deal to the stage where it generates income. I call this return on time invested (ROTI).

The other aspect is risk – the risk that I invest my time and energy and a deal does not complete. Now that risk is ever present, in traditional buy-to-let as well as lease options. I believe the risk that a deal will not complete is greater in a lease option.

Again, this can be explained easily. Think about the types of sellers we might come across in the course of an investment deal; homeowner moving as part of the normal course of life, repossession companies, probates, estate agents and solicitors. These are all 'normal' players in the buying and selling game.

Targeting vulnerable and distressed sellers

A flaw in the lease option strategy is that it requires you to target vulnerable and emotionally distressed sellers. Some people call these people desperate sellers or motivated sellers. The truth is they are in some sort of mess and need help. I think you can already see why this strategy would be attracting attention from the FCA and others.

A lease option deal will definitely take more of your time to reach completion than a straight purchase from an estate agent. Therefore, when I did a time cost comparison I worked out that I could source more deals in one year compared to potential cashflow and capital gain from one lease option!

Let me explain: I could source one property deal per month for a fee of £8,000 each, totalling an income of £96,000.

How many lease options would you need to complete on to get this sort of income? Your only source of income is the rent surplus. On top of this, you will have the costs to arrange, possibly as much as £4,000 in solicitor fees *and* the cost to refurbish the property to a rentable state. Unless of course you hunt for the golden goose. The tenant buyer with trade skills who is prepared to move into a property in a mess and do it up while paying your rent.

If a seller was not in distress, they would sell through an estate agent in the traditional way – so you are going to be explaining a new method of 'not-selling' your home to someone who just wants to get rid of the source of their stress.

If you are truly interested in win-win-win solutions, then great – please help people because there are sellers in a mess. However, take on the property deal in the full knowledge of what you are taking on.

The reality of the process

Prior to working with me a mentee had been following a lease option strategy for a year and only closed one deal worth £200 per month. That was a lot of work for a low return; less than £2,400 a year after costs and also twelve months of no income.

Don't get me wrong, if you do this alongside a job, then you are definitely on your way to early retirement.

In my experience, if you know how to find buy-to-let properties that provide a great cashflow, then why not set up a business doing just that?

You still need to follow investment rules to make a lease option a safe strategy. These include an exit strategy for the deal, profit margins, what happens if interest rates go up, the seller dies before the end of the term or worse goes bankrupt – have you planned for these contingencies?

Deal structure in detail

A purchase option will involve agreement of an 'upfront payment' to the owner (similar to the deposit concept in a normal purchase). Then monthly payments over a number of years, like normal mortgage payments. Finally, at the end of an agreed time, you can purchase the property at a figure that was agreed at the beginning of the contract.

The upfront payment can be as little as £1 if you are negotiating to 'buy' a property using an option, and as much as 5% of the 'purchase' if you are negotiating to sell an option to someone else. In a sense, a lease option is very much like buying a car on lease; you would put down an initial deposit (or maybe trade in your car for a set value) and then make monthly payments.

At the end of the agreed term, you would have the choice to either buy the car for a pre-agreed figure or hand the car back. A lease option on a property is very similar to this.

So to summarise, there are two key parts to the lease option strategy:

1. You could lease the property from a home owner and gain permission to lease the property (i.e. rent it) to another tenant. In effect, you are acting like a letting agent with maintenance responsibilities, but with rights to all the profit from the rent (after the cost of the seller's mortgage, insurance and repairs). Just like rent to rent have you budgeted for the repairs?

2. The other part to the option is agreeing a purchase price with the seller today, with a delayed finalisation of the deal. In effect, you are agreeing the price and the option to buy, but you are not obligated to buy as you would be with an exchange of contracts. This is what most proponents of lease options are focused on.

There are lots of numbers and terms involved, and there are four main figures that you need to consider and negotiate when either entering into or selling an option. Let's make things easier and simply talk about how you can use an option to take control and eventually buy a property. Do remember that this is only one example and options are a useful tool in the professional investor's armoury.

1 Purchase price

One of the most challenging things to consider is the purchase price of the property. As with all deals, you need to know that you are paying a fair price for the property. What is a fair market value?

When you negotiate a traditional buy-to-let purchase, your aim is to buy in equity at the point of purchase, i.e. when you complete on the mortgage, because that is when you are setting the level of the debt. If you agree a price of £100,000, then your debt will be a percentage of that (the LTV you have borrowed) and you will have to pay it back.

So, with a lease option you are effectively agreeing a purchase price sometime in the future. What you are saying to a seller is that you will agree to buy their house today for £100,000, but you will pay them in three, five or 15 years – you choose.

In the meantime, you will (effectively) pay their mortgage and take on responsibility to repair and maintain their home. This means that the seller can move out of the property and move on with their lives, without the financial cost of the property hanging around their necks.

When you negotiate the 'purchase price' you can take the view that you can afford to agree a price close to the asking price because when you finally complete on the deal in, say, three, five or seven years' time, the real value of the property will have increased and you will be buying below future market value.

Circumstances and the homeowner's need to move will impact on their likelihood of agreeing to a current market value purchase price with delayed completion. It depends on the depth of rapport you build with the current homeowner and when they want or need to move out of the property.

2 Timescales or the term of the lease

When negotiating the lease you also ask for the option to buy the house at an agreed time in the future. So, if you are buying a house using an option, it would be a great idea if you could agree to buy the house at today's price and then actually only pay for the house when it has increased in value (thereby gaining the equity we normally look for when buying in the traditional way).

When thinking about the 'term' of the lease you will need an understanding of the property market in your area and for your specific property. If prices are moving well and increasing, then you could agree a shorter time. If prices are moving more slowly, then you might want to agree a longer lease so that you give house prices a chance to recorrect and increase before you are required to complete on the purchase part of the option.

The length or term of the option to buy will be determined in some ways by the price. What you want to achieve is a term for the option that is long enough for the house to increase in value so you can complete, using for example a 75% mortgage, which would cover the full purchase price.

If you agree to buy a house for today's price of £70,000, you need to calculate when you think the property will be worth £100,000. What do you think? Three years? Seven years? Longer? It's quite tricky. That's why you also need to ensure that you have the right to extend the term of the contract in case house prices do not climb as quickly as you thought. The main principle here is to agree as long a term as possible, and then buy sooner if it suits you.

3 The upfront payment (deposit)

An 'upfront payment' can be as low as £1 or if you are really coming from a win-win-win position, it can be enough money to pay the homeowner's rent and deposit on a new property, their removal costs or some other financial cost that they are worried about and need to pay.

This initial payment is totally negotiable and really starts at the point where you understand what the homeowner wants to achieve from their business dealings with you. If they want to move out, that is exactly what you want to achieve as well. Now what needs to happen? Do they need money to move?

If not, then do not feel obliged to offer a large upfront payment.

4 Monthly payments

In most instances, monthly payments are simply the cost of the mortgage payments. Sometimes you come across homeowners who have second loans.

The principle thing to remember is that the potential rent you will get once the property is let out must cover the cost of the mortgage payments now and in the future when interest rates go up, and insurance costs, repairs, maintenance, gas and electrical certificates etc. In the rent to rent strategy these costs remain the responsibility of the owner – you can see how the strategy is already easier.

At this stage things could get complicated. You will need to be good at maths and understand this strategy fully. Make sure that you learn lease options the English way, as our rules and mortgage conditions must be met upfront. The other point to make is the importance of an expert team to support you! The difference between the rent and the mortgage and running costs is your profit.

Who agrees to a lease option?

As I explained earlier, the homeowner is more likely to be in some form of distress. They could also be landlords who might want to have their property let on a long-term basis without the cost of management fees. A landlord might be happy to relieve himself of the responsibility of the property.

And, of course, sellers who can't sell their houses for a number of reasons may be interested in this approach.

Every situation will be different as it depends on the seller's previous experience, what they want the end result to be and in what timescale.

Geographically, this strategy has different results across the country. This strategy can take time, but once the seller understands that you have a good legal team in place and a solid contract, they can become more comfortable with the situation.

Whatever situation the seller is in, they are likely to be more vulnerable and with that comes a professional duty of care. It is your responsibility to be sure that the deal will work for you over the period of the agreement. While you might not have a legal obligation to buy the property, I believe you have a moral obligation to make the payments you agree to – not just do it for a while until it gets difficult and then pull out!

Tenant buyers – the other side of the equation

Putting a tenant buyer into the property, especially someone who is willing to do some work on the property can ensure the property is looked after, as the tenant buyer will treat and maintain the property as if it was their own. This also means that there is regular (almost) guaranteed cashflow coming in.

A tenant buyer is the world's best tenant, and your best asset, as they are not moving into a house, they are moving into their home. The tenant doesn't view the property as a normal rental property. They move in and spend their own money adding value to the property. The tenant builds an emotional attachment to the property. You will need to maintain your relationship with them as they are, in effect, your most valuable asset. After all, you don't own the house.

Like any business, property investors can always get themselves a bad name if they want to. The principle of this strategy is building a relationship with people who are in a difficult situation. They want to move home for some reason and can't. You can help. Build that relationship and find a mutually acceptable way forward.

Think of the seller; don't aim to back them into a corner – keep all the options open. Whatever you do, do it with the seller's interests in mind. If you put a marketing plan together, you might be able to find sellers in this situation. Remember that, above all, have a good legal team behind you, as it is important to get things right from the start.

To summarise

Understand how the strategy works, understand the numbers involved and create your own set of lease-option buying rules. These should include:

- Area and exit strategy.
- Payments, rent and mortgage costs – what's the profit and will it stand an increase in interest (build that into the contract)?
- Flexibility – what if prices go up sooner or, worse, not quickly enough?
- Seller consequences – what if they die or go bankrupt, or never come back? What if they do come back? Have you been fair? Consider a profit share – remember win-win-win.
- Does the time work for you – consider your time investment. Is this a good use of your time?
- Remember the costs involved – marketing upfront, refurbishing the properties to rent, your solicitor, broker fees.
- No matter what they tell you, a lease option is not an asset. The only asset in the deal is your tenant who pays the rent and makes the profit – you are a letting agent!
- No matter what they tell you, selling a lease-option contract to another (foolish) investor is just what the banks did when they sold derivatives of bad debt – there is no asset to sell.
- Consider rent to rent as a simpler route to income.
- In my experience, if you know how to find a deal in a cashflowing area, then simply find people willing to invest – they have a different mindset and marginally less emotional issues to deal with. You will make as much, if not more, money for less stress. Become a property sourcer!

Consequences, risks and income

Find the right deal and you will benefit from the rental profit as a letting agent, just like the rent to rent technique – this will use your personal time but with great systems it can be managed.

The problem for me with this strategy is the time it takes to find and negotiate a deal – with no certainty that it will reach a contractual stage. The legal fees are much higher to effectively tie the seller to the deal – rather than have them as willing and grateful partners. Then there is the risk that you accept a lower income deal in the hope that you will be able to complete on the promised future sale.

At one event I attended the speaker said that every contract they had been due to complete on had to be rewritten by solicitors. That involves more cost, knowing where your seller is, and runs the risk of renegotiation.

Now I totally agree that you should not worry about the cost of the shovel when digging for gold – but I don't want to dig through concrete and I am not sure my golden seam is lying just outside of Tesco's.

I have already explained how much time and money I invested in this strategy with little success. This strategy is ideal if you are a great (and I mean great) sales person. Your ability to communicate with a person in some degree of distress and convince them you are the solution to their problems is pivotal.

There are expensive legal costs and, personally, I would still want a survey (as I am not a builder) to thoroughly check the property that I might buy in the future. This is a time-intensive, costly strategy that is best developed close to home. If you have the time, the skills and the funds then go for it. But as I have already said, I believe rent to rent is easier to sell as a concept and sourcing is a quicker route to more cash.

Leases, options and lease options are a useful tool, but not a primary strategy.

Chapter 16 Assisted sales

In the first edition, I spoke about assisted sales as being a great cash-generating strategy. Effectively, the strategy is to help a seller to sell, as opposed to sourcing which is helping an investor to buy.

During the last couple of years, horror stories of sellers being emotionally devastated by the deals they agreed to have started to float around.

Let's start this whole section by repeating that being an ethical investor is the only way to be. If you don't feel that way, then I guess you would also have stopped reading several chapters back anyway!

We only need a relatively small amount of income to be financially free – for most people £2,000–£3,000 is enough to cover their costs. Double that and you will have a great cashflowing strategy and contingency. If you remember this, then there is no need for you to rush, struggle or bully people.

Assisted sales explained

You might start by attracting private sellers through your marketing. Their situation may mean that the deal does not work for you as the buyer of discounted property. You will have an arsenal of strategies including options and assisted sales as a way to help. Offering a lease option makes you a letting agent. Doing an assisted sale can make you an estate agent.

If the latter is the case, then I feel personally that you deserve a fee for your time, like an estate agent. I struggle to see how acting like the 'House Doctor' as seen on the television means you are entitled to 50% or more of someone's equity from their home, regardless of the financial trouble they were in!

To me, the real idea of the assisted sales strategy is that on your travels you will come across deals that do not work for you as an investor. However, the seller still wants to sell and you could use your knowledge to help them.

The turning point of this strategy is that the property will be a private sale and not already on the market with an estate agent and you will recognise how you could add value to the deal in order to maximise the final sale value. This is way beyond the role of an estate agent – this is a property entrepreneur. You might even use some of your cash to enhance the property through development, an extension or splitting titles.

In some cases, the fees charged have been £10,000s of pounds. A disproportionate fee for the work involved as a house doctor, but a fair profit share to off-set the risk of using your personal cash! There are stories that some sellers have been so emotionally depressed as a result of this type of agreement, made while they were stressed and vulnerable, that they have harmed themselves! Really, is that how you want to do business?

So, if you find a suitable assisted sales property, what might it look like?

Well, it could be a large two-bedroom house that you could reconfigure. It could be a house where there is scope for a loft or rear extension. It could be a large property split into flats, but not under separate titles (Chapter 13 – Splitting). It could be owned by an investor and they might be struggling or over leveraged.

It could be anything where you with your expert knowledge could add significant value for relatively low outlay.

This, like lease options, is a secondary strategy in my opinion. Beware – when a deal does not work for you as a traditional investment deal – question yourself as to whether you have time and experience to pull off an assisted sale and then make your choice. Personally, I would consider offering a fee for my time if I was simply selling, or a profit share if my cash and time added significant value. If making a profit share agreement, personally I would agree a split of 40/60 or even 30/70 in favour of the seller – it is, after all, their home and their inheritance.

Case study

To assist, split, and option

I worked with a mentee who has architectural skills and they found a deal that they knew they could add value to.

The property was a probate and in a desirable area. It needed refurbishing but it could also be enhanced from a two-bedroom property to a four-bedroom.

My mentee built a relationship with the seller, through the estate agent, to the point where the seller was prepared to accept an offer.

Outline plans were drawn, quotes for the renovation and refurbishment project were received and we started to run the numbers for a couple of strategies to fund the deal.

Our options were:

- A lease option to secure the deal and agree the price – not a bad idea as it would secure the deal and, yes, agree the future price. However, we wanted to be clear that our aim was to buy and sell and not get confused with renting, so in fact we just needed an option or a lock out agreement.
- Assisted sale – well, yes, we could assist the seller to achieve a higher valuation but, in this case, the sale was a probate which would mean that the higher end value would create higher inheritance tax liability. There was also an estate agent in the chain of contacts. So, a conversation was held to get them to waive the first set of fees in return for higher end fees when we sold at the new sale price. The danger here was if we couldn't find a buyer.
- To buy outright with commercial funding, bridging or a mortgage with no redemption penalty and low fees. The disadvantage of this strategy was that it required a lot more cash input.

The property

The property was a 1960s two-bedroom split-level house sitting high on a city hillside with stunning views – a much sought after location for those wanting close, easy city access yet stylish seclusion for their home life. This was checked with local estate agents to assess the potential redevelopment value and most importantly demand.

The property was well maintained though dated and ideal for renovation. The layout consisted of a huge open-plan lounge/dining area, with panoramic views on three sides, which led into a large kitchen. There were two bedrooms to the rear with a separate bathroom. At the lower ground level, there was a large double garage plus a workshop.

The house was originally marketed at £320,000. There was a significant amount of work to be carried out for an ordinary purchaser. The estate agent was happy for my mentee to deal direct with the seller (his fee was of course guaranteed no matter what). This spoke of a high level of trust and relationship, which is critical with such a key member of the deal team.

After much negotiation, an initial purchase price of £260,000 was agreed. This was still above the stamp duty threshold – another tax to contend with – so more negotiations were entered into to agree a purchase price and a fee component for allowing a potential delayed completion.

The road on which this property was situated had uniquely designed properties, all individual and therefore difficult to find comparisons for the figures involved. This was to be a challenge throughout the process – but when sold to a member of the general public as their home, their emotions would take over!

Options for development

No permissions were required for the redevelopment, just a Building Regulations application, which the mentee could handle directly. First, the garage and workshop could be converted into two additional bedrooms with either an ensuite each or a shared bathroom. This level would be accessed via a new spiral or standard staircase from the current main living space above. This would create a four-bedroom property and would require the lower level walls to be tanked, floors insulated and windows inserted in place of the garage doors.

A second approach would be to utilise the roof space to create two new bedrooms with ensuite or a shared bathroom with a new staircase from the existing living area. There was ample space as the rooms were large. The lower floor garage could stay in use and the workshop could become a games room.

The exit strategy

The selling agents were confident of a resale price, once the works were complete, of between £370,000 and £400,000. They had previously had a prospective purchaser for the exact property who had £420,000 to spend and would have bought it had it been in an updated state where he could have moved straight in without having to undertake the works himself.

A critical factor in the success in selling this unique deal was the mentee's contacts, they were well connected in circles where potential buyers were likely to come from, for example, the armed forces, business executives and other wealthy individuals. It is vital to know that you are creating a product that you can sell.

We created an ideal scenario which was to market the property as the refurbishment works commenced, having already entered into a lock out agreement with the seller. When the buyer was identified they could then influence the final touches to their own taste and colours, thus providing a unique personal service tailored to their individual requirements.

This became the start of a complete brand – a personalised development service for those who want a quality home but without the hassle of making a house their home. We can make any house your home! The service includes sourcing the property, surveying and planning alterations, dealing with and submitting applications to the relevant local authorities, arranging and overseeing the building and refurbishment works and handing over to the new purchaser.

In the end, the deal worked as follows:

- Initial purchase: price £250,000.
- Fee to seller for delayed completion: £10,000.
- Building budget, including contingency and overrun: £62,000.
- Cost of borrowing on initial purchase price, including fees (£187,500 @ 5.5% for 6 months): £7,500.

- Cost of funding the purchase and rebuild costs were repaid through the profit at the end.
- Resale value: £410,000 (less agent and solicitor fees £7,500).
- Fee for project management: £23,000. (This was how we paid for our time to project manage the process).
- Total cost to buy and renovate: £360,000.
- Profit £50,000. And personal fees £23,000.
- A definite example of using investor and entrepreneurial thinking to create more for everyone.

Consequences of Assisted Sale

This strategy needs you to develop direct marketing with potential sellers, or build a relationship with an estate agent to help move properties that are stuck – that takes time.

Once properties are found that are suitable for you help – work out whether you are offering your expertise and time or your money to make the new sale happen.

Understand the risks and make sure you have agreements that are both fair to the owner and binding to ensure that you do receive your fair fee.

Again a nice strategy to run close to home. Potentially very little financial outlay and perfect if you have the 'eye' of a house doctor.

Chapter 17 Leads and deals

In summary, the principle here is to build your business marketing funnel to such a degree that any spare leads that you generate and can't use for yourself can simply be sold on to someone else. Now comes the tricky bit. How? This is such a broad topic with so many variations I will have to break them down.

Lead-driven vs client-driven approaches

When I talk about lead-driven sourcing I am talking about high numbers of leads generated through internet campaigns, leaflets or newspaper adverts. The medium doesn't matter; the concept is that you, the sourcer or lead seller, are collecting lots of people's names and contact details. You then sell them to a wide audience – you don't necessarily talk to the seller and don't know the potential investor. If you get your system right, you can 'pre-qualify' these leads directly into your database.

Another approach, which I term as sourcing, is where you source or find deals to meet the specific needs of a client or group of clients. This is like shopping to order and is a lower volume and more personal service. I will discuss sourcing in Chapter 18, first let's look at the details of leads and deals and then talk about the strategies behind them.

Selling leads – cold

This strategy requires you to establish a system where you can attract a lot of leads and the most common approaches are internet sites, leaflet campaigns and newspaper adverts. In this model, you sell the 'cold' lead to another investor for something between £25–£100. This strategy is designed to be a high-volume automated business with a relatively low level of overheads depending on your internet marketing skills.

The critical pivot point in this strategy will be your internet marketing and technical skills. If you love the computer and love googling then this could be great for you. You become like a property dating service for people wanting to sell and those wanting to buy.

You could develop this around a Facebook page or even a membership site or group – the choice is yours. I did not follow this approach, apart from a very clear lack of technical skills, I want to know I will be paid for the work I do. You need to realise not every deal you find will be bought.

The other simple challenge that few people promoting this idea actually discuss is that a website is only a valuable resource if it appears on the front page of an internet users search engine when they search certain terms – a tiny yet critical step that definitely requires high internet skills or the money to pay someone who can deliver a 'page one ranking'.

Packaged deals

In this case, you will have had more interaction directly with the seller of the property, maybe visited the house and even agreed a sale price with the seller. Typically, people who sell packaged deals will work with a broker or financial advisor to create a no or low money down way of buying the lead. Now the price charged is closer to £3,000, which may include fees to the broker.

Mark I'Anson is well known in property circles for his skill in building a rapport with potential sellers and agreeing the terms of a deal. He's also the author of *Dominate Your Ground* and agreed to share his four top tips.

Mark and I both agree that no book is for the shelf, they're written so you can start doing. You'll probably make mistakes along the way and Mark admits he made loads, but managing those mistakes is the art. Make your mistakes small and painless, learn from them and do better next time. 'It's called doing and managing mistakes to grow,' says Mark; I think that's a great quote.

Tip 1 Find your ground

Mark recommends that it is good practice to think about your local area, 'I realise that some areas are better than others but, where yields are low, or discounts not quite there, try to think outside the box a little'.

In the old days, a lot of people got into property in an accidental way, they stumbled upon a deal and that got their minds working. 'Could there be more deals like that out there?' asks Mark.

Mark also recommends that it is good practice to work your own area. Trying to manage a patch that's miles away will test you, it's not forgiving, and the travelling doesn't get easier. You should value your time, and travelling takes that time away. It's not productive time either, some will argue that you can listen to CDs and make it productive but, working in your business is productive, driving generally isn't – no matter how you try to justify it.

Think about the wear and tear on you as well as your vehicle and the erosion of your valuable time. You got into this to improve your quality of life, not to buy yourself another job.

If you're serious and genuinely convinced that your area won't work then move into one that does. You are a property person now; we move to suit our business if we need to.

Tip 2 Choose your tactics

Multiple layers of marketing are vital when applying the foundations for marketing for leads, it's important to note that they work together. Mark promises that if you only do one method, you are likely to get few calls and few leads. Marketing is an art form; one method doesn't work better than another in that they all have pros and cons to doing them. Some have costs in time, some in money. These methods cost in money and may also cost in time and effort – make your own decisions on which ones to do first and how much to spend – your budget is your own and only you can tell how much to put into each and when you've run out.

As Mark explains one example is classified newspaper advertising. When dealing with those wonderful 'classified' sales people, it's often frustrating. They promise that your advert will appear on the right-hand facing page of the newspaper (first place people tend to look at) when, in reality, they have no control on layout, editorial has control so, no matter what they say, your advert is going where they put it. Often, and this is the frustrating part, they'll promise again and again giving away free space to compensate when you complain.

Let's deal with this in a slightly different way and save some of the frustration. Accept that you have little or no control over where your small advert is going to appear, once you're over that hurdle, you can work with what you have.

There are myriad opinions on advertising, but the only one that counts on your patch, is yours!

Tip 3 Start with local – stick with local

The problem for a start-up is that the research isn't cheap. Mark has created his own technique and often uses Asda as research. Walk into an Asda store and look at the layout of the store. Mark says, 'I'm from an upper working class/lower middle class background and upbringing, my family is a meat and two veg type family, we don't have soft drinks in the house, we eat sensibly, exercise well and I'd like to think that we were brought up right.'

When checking the layout of the store in your local area, what do you see first? In supermarkets that we shop in, we expect to be greeted with a huge fruit and vegetable section at the entrance. It's inviting, and it seems to make sense to our upbringing. Those stores that have clothing at the entrance, or offers on crates of beer, or a huge pastry section don't seem to look right. So what could you tell about an area from their supermarkets?

Don't take Mark's word for it either, try this for yourself. Have a trip out to a few stores that may open on your patch – you'll be surprised.

Tip 4 Preparation & planning

Okay, you've made an appointment to see the lead. There's some research to do before you visit, most of it can be done online. 'Rightmove, Nethouseprices, MousePrice and Hometrack all offer valuation tools with varying degrees of accuracy and if you're using them you don't know your patch well enough in my opinion.' warns Mark.

If you know your patch, you'll know the ceiling prices on every street, the movers and shakers in the area, the property that sells quickly.

Mark does use the online portals for some information and some checking, but he generally knows a price beforehand. In the north, a two bed terrace will sell for £85k in good condition, slightly cheaper without central heating, even cheaper if it needs a refurbish.

Mark's key tip is to get round your patch and learn the prices:

2 Bed Terrace – mid and end – good condition and refurbishing required – ceiling price on street.

3 Bed Terrace – mid and end – good condition and refurbishing required – ceiling price on street.

2 Bed Semi – good condition and refurbishing required – ceiling price on street.

3 Bed Semi – good condition and refurbishing required – ceiling price on street.

Time and consequences

This form of lead development can either be a business in its own right or a way that you market and find deals (or both). Mark recommends and I agree close to home is best, but knowing your area or patch is crucial (as in all techniques). This will take time to get established – first finding the right area and the right combination of marketing strategies.

Like lease options, this is a technique for the sales person in you. If you cannot sell then this will not work. While you are planning to secure the property to sell as a deal or buy for yourself, you are, in fact, first selling the seller the idea that they need to sell the property to you. This is sales intensive 101!

With all the techniques explained so far. The impact on your lifestyle is mitigated by your area and distance to home, your available cash to invest in the technique, and marketing in relation to the value of your time and income generated. The budget is up to you, if cash is short start with local leaflet drops you deliver yourself, before heading to more expensive newspaper adverts. These could be a waste of time if you have not done your research properly.

But do well and your lifestyle will dramatically improve!

Chapter 18 Sourcing for cash – build a business

There are definite benefits of developing a sourcing business. If you love property, then create a property investment sourcing service – you will need to find deals that specifically match the investment method you are an expert in. Wherever you are based, the draw for investors is cash on cash return – 'what's the ROI?'

A more bespoke service definitely takes more time but is, consequently, worth more as a service. Now you will really need to think about what you have to offer that makes people want your product/service. Think about how you are different, then go and find the investors who need your help.

As I have already mentioned I focus on offering a bespoke service to busy people who recognise the benefit of property investment, but neither have the time nor the knowledge to invest on their own. They have either cash or equity available, and they want a good rate of return on their investment. I specialise in building cashflowing property portfolios in the north of England, which include single lets or properties developed into high cashflowing multi-lets.

My business is all about service, adding value and a great ROI, and return on time investment (ROTI). I charge for my time, knowledge and experience and then use those funds to invest in another property for myself. My model enables me to buy every sixth property for myself using other people's money, or just have another holiday. The best bit is that I am following the same investment and geographic strategy with my clients and my own portfolio. Whether I am buying for myself or whether it is for a joint venture or a client, it's a great use of my time.

The business is all about relationships: first with the investor, to understand why they want to invest and then purposefully going out to source specific deals to meet their needs; and then with the sellers as you maintain contact with them to ensure the completion of the transaction.

You can charge anywhere between £3,000–£10,000, and the service you offer may take your client to the point of purchase or all the way through refurbishment to the signing of the AST.

Picking the right strategy

The right sourcing strategy will depend on your personal investment strategy. If you are happy to buy anywhere in the country, then you will most likely be looking for or generating leads from anywhere in the country. This forms the basis of your business.

Alternatively, if you have a specific niche – like HMOs in one location or cashflowing properties in the north – then your marketing will focus on and generate those specific leads. However, the added value comes when you really specialise and have your own local team. Now you can offer a packaged service and charge a fee by sharing business with your team and leveraging your time.

Making it work in your favour

I believe that if you understand the principles of what makes an investment a great investment (i.e. cashflow and potential capital growth) and how to manage the process, then this business model can easily generate the cashflow that enables you to invest in property using other people's money.

Whether or not you can afford to buy right now doesn't factor into this strategy. You are simply building relationships with estate agents or running your marketing campaign to attract deals. The only extra factor needed is the outlet for the 'spare' deals.

The volume of spare deals depends on whether you are actively buying and the size of your marketing funnel.

As you market to attract properties, you also market or locate the appropriate pool of investors who would want to buy your spare deals – networking perhaps. Then, you offer spare deals and the appropriate level of service to your list of warm investors and charge a fee.

Return on time invested (ROTI)

The easiest example of ROTI is to ask the question: 'How much does this activity earn me in an hour?' It helps, of course, if you know two other figures. First, how much do you need to earn an hour to cover your costs?

And, second, how many hours do you need to work in a time period, day/ week or month? I have talked about your hourly rate in previous chapters – let's run the process on the sourcing business model.

For example, keeping to the same figures I used in Chapter 14 Rent to rent, to earn the equivalent of £36,000 a year (after tax) divide it by 10 to get a monthly figure of £3,600. I chose 10 months as a working period because I want 8 weeks of holidays, including bank holidays. Now think about how many working days in a month you can charge for after marketing, administration and sales. That's two days a week – just 8 days per month. So, divide £3,600 per month by 8 income-generating days on average to get £450 per day.

So, if you worked and invoiced for 8 days per month for 10 months at an income rate of £450 per day, you would earn £36,000 per annum. Now look at this, £36,000 per annum is selling to six bespoke clients at £6,000 each to invest in a cashflowing refurbished property with a tenant in place – could you do that? Or maybe twelve clients at £3,000 each until you gain in confidence and develop your model and systems further.

It is crucial to understand this concept. When you know how much you need to earn to cover your bills and how you can earn it, you will have found the path to financial freedom and it's much easier to get there if you stay on the path! These are just concepts to help you understand the topic – you will need to factor in contingencies and the cost of running your business and tax. Plus, of course, the fact that you would like to earn more than £36,000 per annum!

Consequences, time and lifestyle

- Sourcing enables you to leverage your time and get the best income generation possible by knowing how much you want to earn and how you can earn it.
- You can use your knowledge and experience to help other cash-rich, time-poor investors build cashflowing property portfolios that offer not only great cashflow but also a great ROI, and charge a fee that is in line with your target income.
- Then you can leverage the fees you charge by reinvesting and buying more property into your own portfolio, which in turn produces cashflow. You will have a cashflowing business and accounts so that you will be able to obtain mortgages – a real bonus.

In terms of consequences you need to be professional, trustworthy and transparent in all your dealings with clients. There are certain professional standards you need to adhere to:

- business and professional indemnity insurance,
- membership to the Property Ombudsman Scheme,
- Data Protection standards,
- eventually creating a limited company and registering for VAT.

Staff will also be needed as you grow the business; this means more insurance and contracts and day-to-day accounts, and salary calculations.

The business should grow organically to meet your lifestyle commitments and your income needs. As you decide to take on more business and demand grows then you can find yourself growing a business that moves from lifestyle driven to a proper job – be clear what your personal objectives are.

Chapter 19 Protecting those you love

Did you know that, in the UK, seven out of ten people die intestate (without a valid will)? This means that important decisions on how their assets and possessions are distributed are left to the government to decide under intestacy rules. Many people assume that their spouse or partner will get everything if they die. Unfortunately, this is not necessarily the case. In fact, if you are not married or in a civil partnership, there is a good chance your partner will receive nothing.

This is going to seem like a strange chapter, but I feel that I need to include it. This topic came up quite early on in my personal journey and then really hit home in late 2010 when my best friend died, leaving her family to 'clear up' her property portfolio.

As this whole book is about using other people's money, some of those people will be family and friends who will have worked hard for their money in the first place. Even if you do have a will, how will your beneficiaries benefit from your estate? Will they have to sell the portfolio to raise money (some of which will be needed to pay death duties)?

Why not take out an insurance policy, place it in trust, include it in your will and then at least your family will have a guaranteed sum of cash to work with while they rearrange the finance of the portfolio? They could use the insurance policy to clear the mortgages and keep the properties and the associated income), or they could use the money to recruit a specialist to help them refinance the portfolio – think about it.

If you do already have a will, you need to ensure that it is still valid. For example, marrying or entering into a civil partnership after your will is made will normally revoke it. Alternatively, if you divorce or dissolve your civil partnership after your will is made, your will is not automatically cancelled.

Entering into a business arrangement or partnership may require changes. You need to read and check that your will is still valid.

I was amazed at how easy and inexpensive this process can be: my parents paid over £500 to go to a solicitor; we paid less than half for two wills. Life insurance, again, does not have to be expensive – unless of course you are old or smoke, or both. I had one partnership at the time of writing the first edition where we did not take out insurance. Therefore, at a time of serious illness, we had to get power of attorney to sell the property because we did not plan properly.

All my business partners have now written individual wills and taken out life insurance policies. I am now comfortable that I have protected my property investments, my business and my family will continue to benefit – which is, after all, part of the point.

Will your instructions be followed if you don't have a will?

Epilogue

Seven and a half secrets to using other people's money to invest in property

My aim with this book has always been to share the lessons I have learned about how to successfully invest in property with as many people as possible. I was a university lecturer and I can't let go of the belief that getting an education about a new business is vital to a person's success. I believe knowledge is the new money.

It seems obvious that if you could learn what other people are doing, find out how they did it and what mistakes they made, and then you could create your own even more successful approach.

I speak to so many people who got sucked in by potential 'get rich quick' schemes (I was almost one of them), people who have suffered, been stressed to the point of breaking and lost vast amounts of money. There are many more who started investing to have more time and are now working harder for less.

That's not what I am in business to do – I want to be happy and to leverage my money so that it works and I don't have to. I enjoy spending quality time with my family and friends, that to me is the measure of success.

In the brilliant conversations I have with friends and fellow professional investors I remember so much, learn so much and make more explicit my own learning and understanding of key techniques. Talking to people and learning is crucial. Learn a technique and then dissect it, unpack and take from it those parts that contribute towards your personal journey to financial freedom. Please let me know if I can help you in any way.

There are many more books to come – the next is waiting on my desk as we speak.

I do hope that you benefit from this 'sharing of my knowledge, lessons and mistakes' so that you can go on and create your own even more successful investment strategy. Then, when I write the fourth edition, perhaps you will appear in the book or as a case study sharing your story, knowledge and expertise.

First lesson – develop your personal investment plan

Understand why you are investing and what you want to get out of it.

Understand how much your time is worth and how many hours – billable/ chargeable hours – you need to complete each week to achieve that target.

This income will ultimately come from the properties that you invest in – along the way it will come from the effective use of your time in the right and time-cost effective strategies.

You will have challenges – if you don't, then you aren't doing enough! When those challenges arise, understanding the ultimate vision of your life will pull you through.

I want to scuba dive all the warm waters of the world. The Property Mermaid is a metaphor for me that reminds me of a way of life, one not tied to a desk, freedom and choice being two of my core values. It means fun and adventure and learning new things along the way – more things that are important to me. It means time with my family and friends – without whom we would all be much lonelier!

The strategies and the business must support my life – so they are time effective, cashflowing in a hands-free way through the property portfolio.

When I get bored of diving or just need to dry out, then I have a flexible business model that enables me to work when I choose to. I generate a great return on any of my time that I share with other people either through sourcing, mentoring or strategy sessions. This business generates additional income at a level that is worth my time. My strategies support my desire for an easy, happy and stress-free life.

Pick your financial target, work out what your time is worth and then choose the right strategy for you and your future. Let me know if I can help, I definitely provoke the way people think about investing.

Second lesson – focus

Now you have your personal vision – an idea what you want life to be like – *focus* on it!

Don't allow yourself to be distracted. Be laser-like in your vision and your actions. Yes, of course, still go to networking events – they are crucial. Yes, you will hear the other strategies that people are employing. Remember the amount of income you need. Relax.

With focus, you will achieve your goals. If you constantly flit from one strategy to another, like a poppy in the wind, you will get nowhere. Your journey will be like a ride at a not-so-fun funfair!

Focus

Follow one strategy, implement one technique, listen to others, take pieces of learning and build them into your overall plan and stay *focused*. What more can I say?

Third lesson – know the rules of the game and learn to leverage

From banks to mortgage lenders, credit card companies to family loans, everyone is in business for a reason. Know what they want. Is it as simple as 'interest and charges' on the money they lend you.

You need to understand what they have been saving their money for and in what circumstances would they need their money back. Make sure that you have a plan to return it.

Managing and protecting your credit rating is all part of the same game. Learn how to play the credit card game (see Chapter 4). Learn how to build credit and improve your rating as well as protect your rating. This is an essential business skill that so many property investors still do not understand. Make sure that you are not one of them.

Learn to leverage and make money work for you – there is nothing wrong with that as long as you clearly understand the risks that come with the potential rewards.

Listen to people about the economy, read the right books, learn what caused the current problems and understand the radical solutions being suggested. I highly recommend *Bank to the Future: Protect Your Future Before Governments Go Bust* by Simon Dixon (Searching Finance Ltd, UK).

Fourth lesson – know what your market wants

Knowing your market and what they want is crucial to maximising your profit. So know:

- the difference between preparing a property for sale, as opposed to renting,
- what your family member wants if they lend money to you,
- the terms of any money borrowed from a bridging company.

Tailor everything you do towards your target market – this means refurbishment, redevelopment, marketing and costs. Understand that your strategy and approach will make a considerable difference to the size of your profit margin.

Having said this, always have a second exit strategy in case the property market changes during the process of your refurbishment or redevelopment. Remember how quickly the market turned in 2007–2008 and how many people got caught out.

Make sure you are meeting the needs of your prospective buyer or tenant and not redecorating a 'home' according to your tastes! My tenants love laminate flooring and 'red' or 'blue' bedrooms for the football fans in the house. That's their choice – it's their home.

Fifth lesson – know the difference between a big portfolio and financial freedom

This is really the most important lesson. Lots of people can articulate how many houses they want (or have), some can tell you what cashflow they need to be financially free, but the crucial question is what will you do when you are financially free? You can all guess that I will be scuba diving until I am wrinkly or sucking the rust out of the oxygen tank. The key to success is visualising what your life will be like when you have all the income you need.

Then calculate this to a monthly cashflow target and work to that. I am so often asked, 'How many properties do you own?' What does that matter?

The questions should be:

- Do you have to work for cash anymore?
- How did you become financially free?
- Will you show me how?

My big 'why I invest in property' (apart from it makes so much financial sense) is that I want lots of holidays travelling the world and diving in all the warm waters I can find. I love taking underwater photographs. Bob and I share this passion and what nicer way to live life than to share a passion with someone you are passionate about? I really am very fortunate.

Of course that is just what my cashflow brings me – freedom and the choice to spend my time as I want. My long-term aim and why is to provide a financially independent future for my family and myself. I worked out how much income I needed in three levels: basic costs, contingency and financial freedom. I then set about generating that income.

So what's more important – the size of your portfolio or your happiness?

Sixth lesson – take responsibility for your financial future

I really started to explore this concept as I wrote my second book, *Make More Money from Property: From investor thinking to a business mindset.*

I recognised consciously what I knew subconsciously – that potential economic crises are backed-up waiting to burst into a brand-new day and that I needed to prepare myself and my family to become self-sufficient. In this interdependent world, one country's struggle is another country's recession!

I am already self-sufficient and, in my old age, I will pass on a large cashflowing portfolio to my children and grandchildren to provide for their future comfort and independence. I will take advice on the best way to do this but, in the meantime, I am insured.

What provisions are you making? What happens when you get old? Are you heading for an NHS nursing home where you will sit in a stinky chair rocking as you watch daytime television? Or will you own your own nursing home and have a penthouse (ground floor) luxury apartment waiting for you funded by your shrewd investment decisions.

I plan to slide into my grave shouting, 'Whoopee, what a ride!' Having lived a colourful, and full life as I travel my wavy line from cradle to grave, not a thin, straight, grey and black line of boredom and reliance on the government.

Seventh (and a half) lesson – take action

So you've read this book. Maybe you have done some training before; maybe you still have courses to do? That is great, but what action are you taking?

What's your plan – can I help?

- What is your financial strategy?
- Do you have the clear vision to understand where the money is in the deal?
- Have you calculated the numbers, your financial freedom target, the value of your time, your ROI rules?
- Do you have cash to invest or are you using other people's money?
- What is your investment model?
- Where are you going to invest?
- What will influence that decision?
- Do you have a job or are you doing this full time?
- What is your strategy and where will it work best?
- What is your business model?

Just stop making excuses and get on with it. Find an area and research it. If it works, great. If not, find another one. If you are confused by all the training, then get a copy of *Make More Money from Property: From investor thinking to a business mindset* and follow Section 3 step by step and get out there!

That's why it's only half a secret – because you really should know this by now!

Summary of the summary

The words that I keep repeating are 'purpose', 'gratitude' and 'focus'. Maybe you hear another message. I believe the most important thing is to learn from other people's mistakes – then avoid them and create even easier paths to financial freedom and success. That, of course, is why I wrote this book.

What motivates me through the tough times and the easy times?

As I rewrite this final section, I have just returned from three weeks travelling in Australia. One magical week watching the Northern Lights in Norway and a week in the Maldives snorkling with manta rays.

I have said before that I was a university lecturer for a number of years and I loved that job. I never questioned what I learnt, how my boss treated me, the hours I put in. My pleasure and total satisfaction came from the role of sharing knowledge with other people – helping them to understand something they did not know before.

What is your cup of tea?

My life might not sound like fun to you and that might be because we share different values. Some people would enjoy staying home with close family, and others would love to shop for fast cars or the latest technology.

I am not excited by material possessions. Although, I will admit that last year I bought my first frivolous possession – a car. Yes, I negotiated and bought an ex-showroom model to mitigate the devaluation.

Why am I telling you this?

Because this is what motivates me – the freedom to have amazing adventures, the freedom to travel around the world to see friends, the chance to see wild animals in their natural habitats, to dive with sharks and to learn about different cultures.

For me, 'every day is an epic adventure' waiting to be discovered. Every day is fun (although sometimes tiring and hectic too).

Goals and reasons why

I can't remember exactly where I first heard about making 'your why big enough'. It could have been at my first personal development event in 2007. I don't think I really understood what they meant. Sure, I understood the words but not the meaning behind them. They spoke about positive motivations and towards (rather than away from) motivation. For example, a positive motivation is saying something like 'I want to be thin' rather than 'I don't want to be fat'.

I won't explain all the NLP and psychology behind it. If you are interested, go along to an event for yourself or read books on the topic.

To summarise, a positive statement can be a powerful attraction for you to work towards. If you think of 'why' you want to invest, make the statement personal and positive and it will have a powerful effect in supporting you to reach your goals even more quickly.

For just over four years I have written my goals every November/December in preparation for the next year (I also review them quarterly and monitor them monthly and weekly). Alongside each goal, I have a column that explains or records why this goal is important to me. My 'why' is full of passion, colour and adventure and by writing it down I can't help but be excited and motivated by it.

What I do is not unique; in fact, I would not hesitate to say that every successful investor (or business person) has written powerful goals that shape their progress each day – that guide them towards the outcomes they want to achieve.

I am also not perfect and I have days when I am not as efficient or as focused as others. This is why I have a coach who I speak to regularly to make sure I do stay on track or get help if I am stuck. This brings us full circle to the philosophy of Jeff Olson, who I mentioned in Chapter 1. Every day I make the right choice and I am taking another step towards my goals.

Longer term financial plans: 2014 and onwards

It's great to have the opportunity to look back and review what you have said about your goals in the past. In a video for the Berkshire Property Meet in 2010, I said I didn't want to run a business. That's now not true, but by saying it I have been able to review and refine my thoughts.

A large part of my business now is finding properties for clients, so that they can have cashflowing portfolios without the work. I do all their negotiations and project management for which I charge a fee. In effect, I exchange my time for cash, which creates an ongoing 'wage'. I choose to do this with clients whom I like and when I want to 'work'. The one downside of financial freedom can be boredom. My business allows me to: have fun, meet people, help people, receive financial reward for valuable exchanges with knowledge shared and value created.

I also spend time with clients who want me to help them learn to become a professional investor in their own right, offering coaching and mentorships. This, again, is like a 'wage' as I exchange my time for money.

My immediate plan for the next two years is to focus on achieving the quantifiable goals I have set myself for my business. I have targets set for the 'wages' (time exchanged for cash income), which I can generate through strategic business planning sessions, sourcing and project managing the purchase of cashflowing properties for clients, and mentoring clients who want to become more successful in their own businesses by increasing their accountability.

I will continue to buy investment properties using the strategies described in this book. Primarily, my attention is and always will be on investing in property. I am working on a new strategy in the north west and converting a number of my own properties to test out the system, before I share it with clients.

Building a bigger business

I am definitely not planning any more forays into multi-level marketing and, if you hear me say I am, please come and kick me in the shins! Hard!

Focus is my secret weapon – the way to find the easier path to financial freedom. Why would I want to get off?

I explain my businesses in more detail on pages 159–162, but they are all about property: property investment, property mentoring, developing property business plans and strategies.

And of course more books.

I just love it, love it, love it

Networking and speaking events will continue to provide me with opportunities to both share my experiences and attract new clients and investors. I love meeting people and property networking events are almost becoming part of my social life, not surprising really when property investment is such an integral part of my life. It is not like having a job; I am truly the master of my own destiny. Every decision I make, every action I take (sounds like lyrics to a song – ha ha!) contribute towards my success and the guarantee of a future full of fun, friends, adventures and excitement. Who could ask for more?

I would like to ask a couple of favours

First, if you have enjoyed reading this book and found it valuable, then please tell other people about it and direct them to www.TheSourcersApprentice.com and subscribe to receive our newsletter.

Second, if you would like to leave a comment about the book, then please do: either on my Facebook page or, and of course, an Amazon review which would be like a gold star!

Final thanks

I would like to end by acknowledging all the people who have supported, contributed and worked with me to make this third edition of *Using Other People's Money: How to invest in property*, possible. Liz Harwood and Sue Richardson are two fabulous ladies that helped me produce the first and then second and third editions of this book. Then I just want to say thank you to everyone who has been such a huge support or an inspiration in one way or another. I am eternally grateful and honoured to know them.

I want to offer special thanks and gratitude to Francis and Emily Dolley, Kevin Wright and Mark I'Anson for contributing their tips, knowledge and case studies to this book. I would also like to say thank you to you, the reader. I am honoured that you are reading my words and are interested in my experiences.

I look forward to meeting you and reading your feedback and comments.If you prefer, you can email me directly at the address below. I look forward to hearing from you. Once again, thank you.

Vicki Wusche

The Property Mermaid

Vicki@Wusche-Associates.co.uk

Glossary

Amortization: a commercial lending term meaning the loan 'capital' will be repaid over a specific time period, unlike interest-only mortgages where only the interest is repaid and the initial loan borrowed is still outstanding at the end of the time period.

Annual net income: rent (minus costs such as letting agent fee and insurance) divided by the total amount of money invested into a deal including all buying costs (like solicitor fees, surveys, etc.).

Asset: an investment that generates a profit – puts cash in your pocket.

AST: an assured shorthold tenancy agreement – a contract between landlord and tenant explaining responsibilities and duties. Usually written for a period of six months, though can be longer.

Bad debt: a loan of some form to purchase a product or service that either immediately loses value (e.g. a new car) or continues to cost you money (e.g. buying an item using a credit card and not clearing the bill so that the item then costs 20%+ each month).

Base rate: the rate of interest set by the Bank of England on a monthly basis, by which our whole economy is effectively governed. This is a fiscal tool used to control inflation or stimulate the economy.

BMV (below market value): a specific term meaning a strategy that relies on getting a specific property valuation at a point in the future, to enable all capital invested in a purchase to be recouped or released.

Bridging finance: a specific source of secured funding that some investors use to fund certain deals that require a quicker remortgage or are not eligible for mortgaging. This is an expensive source of funding and requires specialist advice.

Buy-to-let (B2L): the process of buying a property with the intention of renting it to a third party to make a profit from the rent paid.

Coverage: a term used by lenders relating to the percentage of the mortgage cost that is covered by the rental income. Typically 125%: the lender would want your prospective rental income to be at least £125 for every £100 of expected mortgage repayment cost. This figure is set to allow for additional costs to the property such as letting agent fees, insurance, maintenance and void costs. It is a measure of affordability.

Credit scores: a system used by credit-rating agencies. They calculate and attach a numerical value to you based on the risk you pose to lenders. The higher the score (top score 999), the better potential client you are. The lower the score, the worse risk you present to a lender. The risk is whether you will default on your payments.

DIP (decision in principle, also known as agreement in principle): the first stage of the buy-to-let mortgage application process. The lender will assess in broad terms whether or not they want to lend to you as an individual, based on an outline of the loan requirement. They use basic information from an initial application submitted by your mortgage broker and a credit check. The next stage is a full application form and survey.

EPC (energy performance certificate): legal requirement on any property being sold or rented.

ERC (early redemption charge): liable if you redeem a mortgage sooner than an agreed date.

Financial association: the linking of two or more people through the credit reports because of shared borrowing. So a husband and wife, or partners will have a financial association if they both have their names on a mortgage.

Financial statement: this is not a bank statement; this shows your total assets, your liabilities, your income and expenses.

Flipping: to buy a house with the intention of selling it on quickly for a profit. So, to buy it and then flip it back on to the market for sale at a higher price. Another term is 'buy-to-sell', meaning the same principle strategy.

Gearing: a term that states how much you have actually borrowed, particularly on unsecured lending like credit cards, against how much available credit you have. Add up the total debt on all of your credit cards and divide it by the total of all your credit limits. This gives you a percentage – you want your gearing ratio (percentage) to be as low as possible.

Good debt: a term to describe 'borrowing' for the purposes of cashflow. In other words, a 'good debt' is one that puts money in your pocket – one that generates an income.

HMO (house of multiple occupancy): often student housing or professional multi-lets. Each council will have their own area-specific requirements, but broadly any property over three storeys high with three or more unrelated occupants will be eligible for licensing.

Investment strategy: this can be a way to describe the type of properties you buy. For example, buy-to-let or HMOs. It can also describe the type of investment technique being used, for example lease options.

Joint venture: usually refers to a business agreement to access someone else's cash for investment purposes – these are now under strict legislation.

Lease option: a specific strategy aiming to control rather than own an asset or property. Popular in land and commercial deals – it has become popularised in the UK and, like other more 'unusual' schemes, it is under the watchful eye of the Financial Standards Authority. Eventually this will become a licensable strategy.

Leverage: the concept of taking a resource and multiplying the effect it can have. An example is buying a property using a mortgage where, for a fee, a lender supplies some of the capital required. Another example is outsourcing where a person supplies time in return for a fee.

Liability: an investment or purchase that costs you money on a monthly basis – takes money from your pocket.

LIBOR (London InterBank Offered Rate): the interest rate that banks pay for the money they borrow.

Loan to value (LTV): refers to the percentage of the purchase price that a lender is prepared to lend. For example, 75% LTV means they will lend £75,000 out of the £100,000 needed to buy a property, and you need to supply the remaining £25,000 as a deposit.

Market value: could be the price a property is offered for sale, *but* is more accurately the price paid for properties. This information can be found on sites such as Nethouse Price and MousePrice. Ultimately, the price you pay for a property is its market value, even if the house next door is identical and worth more.

No money down (NMD): a strategy popular in 2008 to early 2010 where through various schemes 'deal makers' sought to offer properties for sale for a fee (to them), but no cash was actually required to purchase the house. The properties were then highly leveraged and often low or negative rent producing.

No money left in: the aim to buy a property and enhance its value so that at the point of remortgage you are able to release all of the initial capital that you invested – leaving none of your own money in the deal.

Pay rate: a term used in banking to mean the amount of percentage above base rate that the lender will charge you – in some senses, their profit margin.

Refurbishing: a term used to describe the redecoration of a property to bring it to the standard required by either a rental or sale market.

Rightmove: a well-known website that advertises property for sale or rent – it can be used to assess valuations and rentals. It is also possible to make assumptions about supply and demand in an area.

ROI (return on investment): a useful tool to compare the benefit of investing in one specific asset compared to another, or compared to leaving funds in the bank.

ROTI (return on time invested): a tool to identify the real profit in a specific action, by including the cost of your time to ensure that a deal or purchase actually completes.

Term: how long you borrow the funds for. In some circumstances, this can be limited by age.

Yield: a figure to describe the average return possible based on gross figures.

Bibliography

Publications

Canfield, J. (*et al*) (2009) *Chicken Soup for the Entrepreneur's Soul: Advice and Inspiration on Fulfilling Dreams*, Health Communications.

Dixon, S. (2012) *Bank to the Future: Protect Your Future Before Governments Go Bust*, Searching Finance Ltd.

Hill, N. (1960) *Think and Grow Rich*, Highroads.

Howard, C. (2005) *Turning Passions Into Profits: Three Steps to Wealth and Power*, John Wiley & Sons.

Howard, C. (2009) *Instant Wealth Wake up Rich!: Discover The Secret of The New Entrepreneurial Mind*, John Wiley & Sons.

I'Anson, M. (2013) *Dominate Your Ground*, Berforts Information Press Ltd.

Kiyosaki, R. (2002) *Rich Dad Poor Dad: What the Rich Teach Their Kids About Money That the Poor and Middle Class Do Not!* Time Warner.

Kiyosaki, R. (2009) *Rich Dad's Conspiracy of The Rich: The 8 New Rules of Money*, Hachette.

Kiyosaki, R. (2011) *Unfair Advantage: The Power of Financial Education*, Plata Publishing.

Maxwell, J. C. (2007) *The 21 Irrefutable Laws of Leadership: Follow Them and People Will Follow You*, Thomas Nelson.

Olson, J. (2005) *The Slight Edge: Turning Simple Disciplines into Massive Success*, Momentum Media.

Redfield, J. (1994) *The Celestine Prophecy*, Bantam.

Rohn, J. (1993) *The Art of Exceptional Living* [Audiobook], Nightingale Conant.

Singer, B. (2008) *Little Voice Mastery: How to Win the War Between Your Ears in 30 Seconds or Less and Have an Extraordinary Life*, Xcel Holdings.

Trump, D. and Kiyosaki, R. (2006) *Why We Want You to Be Rich: Two Men – One Message*, Rich Press.

Upton, D. (2009) *Create Your Desires and Fulfill Your Dreams*, UK, unpublished manuscript.

Weerasinghe, R. Dr (2011) *Turning Point: A 6 Step Process for Transforming Your Life*, Ecademy Press.

Wusche, V. (2012) *Make More Money from Property: From investor thinking to a business mindset*, SRA Books.

Weblinks to Vicki Wusche

LinkedIn: www.linkedin.com/pub/vicki-wusche/21/494/4a2

YouTube: www.youtube.com/thepropertymermaid

Facebook: www.facebook.com/VickiWusche

Twitter: www.twitter.com/VickWusche

www.ThePropertyMermaid.com (the blog)

www.ThePropertySourcers.com (for those with cash to invest)

www.TheSourcersApprentice.com (for those who want to learn more about property investing)

Moving forward

Programmes, products and services

I believe it is my purpose in life to share knowledge and, in doing so, inspire and educate people so that they can identify and leverage their previously untapped personal resources. Together, we will create generations of financially secure business owners and property investors and turn our economy back from recession.

I have the writing bug and I will continue to create a variety of books, blogs, products, services and events.

You will find many free resources on my websites, including a free newsletter focused on financial news, property investment and wealth creation.

Visit: www.TheSourcersApprentice.com/free-newsletter

Vicki Wusche

Since 1994, Vicki has shared her knowledge and understanding of all things entrepreneurial, wealth and personal development. She has trained or spoken in front of thousands of people across the UK. In 2013 Vicki was recognised by *The Telegraph* as one of the UK's top 25 most influential people in property.

During her time working at a high level to influence education policy and teaching, Vicki worked with inspirational entrepreneurs at the cutting edge of a new media revolution, while at the same time supporting some of the most deprived people in London through her work as director for two charitable organisations focused on regeneration, housing, refugees, employment and reinspiring young people.

Throughout her time working in education, and more recently in property investment and wealth creation, Vicki has constantly studied both formally and informally the great minds, concepts and strategies vital to business success. This has led to a Master's Degree, a Diploma in Higher Education and a Master NLP qualification to mention but a few.

In 2006, Vicki was made redundant and decided to step out as a full-time consultant. After working almost a year on a freelance basis, the challenges of self employment led her, again, to immerse herself in self-development, which she now points to as the reason for her success.

During 2007, Vicki's attitude towards money changed dramatically as she recognised the power of leverage, the value of her time and how to maximise the return on her investments. Armed with this new understanding in 2008, what seemed an easy process to learn the mechanics of property investing was, again, an interesting experience, as challenge after challenge presented itself as she identified and 'tried' to buy investment properties.

January 2009 saw a dramatic turning point as Vicki recognised she either was going to make a success of property investing or find a job stacking shelves!

The next 12 months saw her buy on average two properties per month and start her sourcing business. By 2010, Vicki's desire to share her knowledge and understanding of property investing and using other people's money led her to publish the first edition of this book.

March 2012 saw the launch of *Make More Money from Property: From investor thinking to a business mindset.* In August 2012 the second edition of this book was published and by November 2012 Vicki was launching her third book called *Property for the next generation: Preparing your family for a wealthy future* at the Business Show. Vicki freely admits she now has the writing bug and is in the process of writing her fourth book.

Throughout her employment and entrepreneurial endeavours, the driving forces behind Vicki are her family and her desire to help others maximise the resources they have, whether they are mental, emotional, financial or physical.

Combining all her skills and experience, with an ability to translate complex concepts with passion into every day practicalities, Vicki is focused on building property portfolios for clients who have access to financial resources. Vicki's clients recognise that this is a once in a generation opportunity to build long-lasting financial security for their families and to secure and leverage their hard-earned wages before inflation erodes them. The clients, however, simply lack the time to take advantage – that's where Vicki's experience and service comes into play.

Together with her business partners, Vicki offers a range of support for those looking to build their own business in property or expand their commercial businesses.

The Property Sourcers

- Do you want to get paid to live in your home?
- Do you want 104% interest on your money guaranteed?

If you are asset or equity rich but time poor, this is your opportunity to build wealth! After experiencing a personalised strategy session, your financial and investment plan will be clearly defined. Depending on your circumstances, personal choice and financial situation, we can take the hard work out of investing for you. We will produce and fully micro-manage an investment portfolio strategy on your behalf, which will allow you to reap the benefits and financial rewards without the effort!

creating your property nest egg

Since 2009, Vicki has been using her experience and knowledge of the property market to build cashflowing property portfolios for bespoke clients.

Offering ROI of over 10%[8], the properties that Vicki sources are identified to generate cashflow and create financial security for clients, leaving them to focus on their lives.

During 2011, Vicki was able to secure access to a unique investment opportunity and, together with her contractors, can now also provide guaranteed high returns of 10–15% for specific clients who meet the investment criteria. Investment opportunities start as low as £30,000 per property and average £65,000 per property.

The process will start with you working together to develop your personal investment plan in a one-to-one strategy session. During a two hour session Vicki works with you to help you recognise the pros and cons of property

---

8   Interest rates, ROIs and guarantees are property specific and subject to your personal financial circumstances.

investment, recognise your personal investment goals and identify a clear investment strategy. While the majority of clients (over 80%) go on to invest with Vicki, this is not a sales pitch. You will leave with a clear investment strategy that enables you to make the right investment choices, at the right time, for you.

With the development of The Property Sourcers, Vicki and partners can now work with a discrete group of cash-rich investors offering a hands-free process designed to balance the investor's needs for security and flexibility with a busy life. They aim to place just 12 of these unique properties over the next 12 months with a further 24 traditional buy-to-let properties.

This service is not for everyone; clients will need to pass credit checks, have a provable income and have access to financial resources. Professional advice will be provided throughout the process through a team of experts in the property, tax and financial world.

With lending criteria becoming increasingly challenging, please contact Vicki and her team to arrange a free, no-obligation call to assess whether this programme suits your needs and circumstances and takes away your worries and concerns. Then book your strategy session to determine your Personal Investment Plan.

For further information on this service, visit www.ThePropertySourcers.com or email Vicki@Wusche-Associates.co.uk to arrange your personalised 'Personal Investment' strategy session.

The Sourcer's Apprentice

- Do you want to start your own property business?
- Did you enjoy reading this book and wish to implement it straightaway?
- Do you feel that you still want even more detail and a step-by-step process to create your cashflowing sourcing business?
- Could you be making even more money from your property knowledge using other people's money?

Vicki and Loran

Vicki recognises that even though she explains the importance of leverage and ROTI, some people still want to create their own property investment business – just as Vicki has done. They have a passion for property and enjoy the houses, the numbers, the challenges and the excitement.

Based on her education, background and experience, Vicki knows that the next best thing to immersing yourself in a live programme is watching and copying those steps in real time through video and audio programmes or joining a mentoring programme.

The Sourcers Apprentice programmes consist of audio, video and workbook solutions to help you rapidly build a successful property investment business. Join us with this informative, in-depth and incredibly valuable multi-learning tool, which takes you from the fundamental inspiration stage right through on a step-by-step learning process to the successful creation of your own personalised business model. Providing you with all the documents, research tools, do's and don'ts, plus hand-holding instructional information to enable you to become a highly effective, cashflowing and profitable property sourcer.

'Become a Property Sourcer in 21 days' is a 6 part online course delivered with homework into your inbox over 21 days. High powered and intense, this course really focuses your mind and tests if you have what it takes to be successful.

'The Business of Investing; Deal Analysis Workshop' is a 2 hour DVD taking you through the ins and outs of Excel, deal analysis and the dreaded maths of working out if you are going to make a profit.

Plus lots more available on our website.

The books, videos and audios enable people to use the learning outlined in this book and in *Make More Money from Property: From investor thinking to a business mindset* and take it to another level. For further information please visit www.TheSourcersApprentice.com.

Check out Vicki Wusche's other books!

Make More Money From Property

From investor thinking to a business mindset

One of The Telegraph's Most Influencial People in Property

'*More Money from Property: From Investor Thinking to a Business Mindset*
is a breath of fresh air, it is honest and truthful about what it takes to
be a success in your finances. Vicki understands it takes more than just
information but a knowledge of how to implement the actions that will
bring success. This deals with the whole and not just a slice of what it
takes to make it in property investing and to some degree life. Highly
recommended.'

Denzil (former mentee)

Property for the
Next Generation

Preparing your family for a wealthy future

VICKI WUSCHE

One of
The Telegraph's
Most Influential
People in Property

'This is a very thought-provoking book and highlights some important issues that every parent should be considering. As someone whose second child is just buying their first house I know the problems that can exist. If you want your children to be able to afford to buy a property then read this book – whatever age your children are now. If you have ever thought property is "out of your reach" then this book will set you straight and help you get a leg on the ladder. Full of good advice with a no-nonsense approach.'

David J Millett (Amazon review)